Lucifer Is At The Helm

Deluxe Edition

AKTAR: Pleiadian Light Warrior

"Many people, especially ignorant people, want to punish you for speaking the truth, for being you. Never apologize for being correct, or for being years ahead of your time. If you're right and you know it, speak your mind. Even if you are a minority of one, the truth is still the truth."

- Mahatma Gandhi

"That which can be destroyed by the truth, should be."

- P.C. Hodgell

"Everyone is entitled to his own opinion, but not to his own facts."

- Daniel Patrick Moynihan

"Those who do not move will not notice their chains."

- Rose Luxemburg

"One of the most cowardly things ordinary people do is shut their eyes to the facts."

- C.S. Lewis

"Facts are stubborn things; and whatever may be our wishes, our inclinations, or the dictates of our passions, they cannot alter the state of facts and evidence."

- John Adams, 2nd President of the USA

"To argue with a person who has renounced the use of reason is like administering medicine to the dead."

- Thomas Paine

"Run not from the darkness. Shield your eyes not from the light. Embrace the darkness as much as the light, for does the light not cast a shadow? Both are one and the same, separate yet joined. As left and right, male and female, up and down, are light and dark, without one the other can have no meaning, as they are but two phases of the same energy. Know that in darkness there is light and in light there is darkness and embrace both equally."

- Liber Umbrarum et Lux (The Book of Shadows and Light)

Lucifer is at the Helm

The world is in trouble. There is a grand conspiracy at work. Luciferian secret societies have taken just about absolute control of the planet. They're using multiple mind-control techniques and they've gained control of almost the entire populace. They've lied about historical events, orchestrated wars as theatrical events while funding all sides simultaneously, created false flag terror attacks, school shootings, bombings and the like. They **LIE** in news broadcasts and history books, medical colleges and institutions. *I have proof!* They've been feeding the population chemicals and toxic germ warfare in their food, air and water in order to give the people cancer intentionally. They poison the underground water reservoirs and wells with chemical fracking, and the press is silent about Fukushima's massive radioactive leak. Americans are being poisoned on all fronts and they are hiding the numerous cures for cancer[1] and other diseases while they kill us with toxic poison in disguise as medicine; most of the so-called "medicine" is toxic deadly, nitrogen mustard gas from WWII is in chemotherapy, cancer enzymes, SV-40 Monkey virus along with a long list of carcinogens are in vaccines! First, they give you cancer and then they put you six feet under with chemo[2]. This is the method of extermination that is being used. Hitler used ovens, these people are using biological warfare and hiding numerous cures[3] for disease! **URGENT! THIS IS AN EMERGENCY! MAY I HAVE YOUR ATTENTION PLEASE!?**

It's really hard not to notice how brainwashed the general American populace is these days and how terribly unreasonable they are in their belief systems. Anything that contradicts the official government version or their spoon-fed religious beliefs is immediately mocked and ridiculed without proper examination. There is a myth going around that the internet isn't a reliable source of information. Everyone has a cell phone that makes pancakes and

---

[1] www.cancertutor.com

[2] https://www.cureyourowncancer.org/chemo-kills.html

[3] www.thetruthaboutcancer.com

scratches your back now and *Google* is right there at your fingertips. There's no excuse not to use available resources. But you do have to dig a little bit deeper than *Google* or *WikiPedia* and you do have to cross reference your resources. Fact checking is the name of the game. If it doesn't hold up, don't believe it until it can be verified true. Pretty simple. Surfing away from *Google* on sites related to the information you're researching is much better sometimes because *Google* censors information. Quite frequently I'll surf off to deep and remote sites on the internet and find things that never show up on *Google* search. Many of these sites have credible and cross-referenced information that pans out to be true under heavy scrutiny. If you learn how to cross check facts and data and learn how to look for more resources, you can't be steered wrong on the internet. It's called knowing how to do research properly. Common Americans consider *WikiPedia* to be research these days. They try to use *WikiPedia* for evidence all the time with me online, with no other verifiable source or reference to back up what it says. Sometimes *WikiPedia* doesn't even reference anything. It's there on *WikiPedia* but there's no source link or cross reference page. Nothing else to go on. In other words, it's not verifiable. It's not real research. Things need to be cross referenced! People in general say that the truth is a wonderful thing, but then they don't even bother to learn how to do research properly so that they can find out what's true, and they despise people who point it out to them. Ask 100 people on the street what they think of things like honesty and truth and 100 of them will say that those traits are virtuous, deserving of great praise. Nobody will say anything bad about honesty or truth. Ever! It's pretty much unanimous regarding those things, and rightly so. But the problem is that the vast majority of people don't appreciate the truth one bit. To the contrary, it most generally pisses them off. The last thing people want to hear about is the truth and they'll argue with you until they're blue in the face. If it contradicts what they've been taught previously by society's institutions, well then forget it, for most typical Americans there's simply no changing it. They'll cling to what they think they know (the official line on everything) and deny everything else in a totally illogical and brainwashed fashion. They've been taught that 2+2=17 and they'll go to their grave believing it, even if it's proven untrue, because that's what Uncle Sam and their preacher told them to believe.

"They must find it difficult... Those who have taken authority as the truth, rather than truth as the authority." **- Gerald Massey, Egyptologist**

That's the sad reality of this country and the state of consciousness that the majority of Americans are in today. As a matter of fact, scientists have recently reported a new strain of fact resistant humans.[4] The article is a parody, but when it comes to reality, umm, it's not a joke. It's the truth. You've all been

HYPNOTIZED!

The classic traits of common American people are that they <u>don't listen</u> and they <u>argue</u> in the face of facts and empirical evidence which are <u>classic signs of hypnosis</u>.

I'm here to tell you that your government is full of shit and that 2+2=4! What the government says is irrelevant, as a matter of fact, if the government says something, you can almost always count on the exact opposite being true! Truth tellers are labeled derogatory terms like conspiracy theorists meanwhile facts and evidence are totally ignored. It's a might-makes-right society, the official line is their Lord and Savior and anyone who questions it gets burned at the stake.

---

[4] https://www.newyorker.com/humor/borowitz-report/scientists-earth-endangered-by-new-strain-of-fact-resistant-humans

If what you say goes against society's myths plan on being a very unpopular person regardless of any facts or evidence that you might have on your side! Plan on being hated by the majority, not because you're wrong, but because you're right. People do not want the truth anymore! In the world of logic and intelligence, ignorance is OK. Being unaware of something is permissible. Arguing with facts and evidence is not! That's not permitted in the world of logic as you'll see in my presentation of the Ten Commandments of Logic at the end of the chapter. Everybody thinks that they know something about something, yet when a simple request for evidence comes in, they get pissed off. I'm constantly scolded online when I make requests for evidence. Umm, why is that? A guaranteed way to piss off the average American is to ask them if they have any *evidence* for what they believe to be true. You're guaranteed to get a negative response in that situation. They'll consider you a rude person immediately simply because you asked for evidence. Perhaps if there's no evidence for what you believe then maybe it's not true? Has that thought ever crossed the minds of brainwashed Americans? Why do Americans get pissed off so quickly when they can't back up what they believe in? Maybe they should hold different beliefs then! Maybe facts and evidence should be their first priority instead of their last!

"When they think they know the answers,
people are difficult to guide.
When they know they do not know,
people can find their own way."
- Tao Te Ching, Ancient Chinese Spiritual Text, Verse 65[5]

The ancient wisdom points out that maintaining an open mind is the way to enlightenment. If you're arrogantly insisting that you're right all the time, you'll get absolutely nowhere! But if you're reaching towards knowledge and wisdom, and are open and dedicated to learning and growing, then you'll be an open channel and you'll evolve quickly. But if you choose to shut yourself off from new information due to arrogance and/or denial you'll forever live in ignorance. I only know what I know until I see facts and evidence to prove otherwise. I'm always open-minded about evidence. If some piece of evidence comes along and says:

"Hey! It's time to wake up now! Here you go, this piece of information is for your growth and knowledge!"

...I'll happily look, listen and pay attention! I'm always open to looking, no matter what it is, until I get to the bottom of it with facts and verified information. But I never, ever scoff and ignore anything. I always investigate. I'll look at the evidence and weigh it logically. If it holds up under scrutiny, I'll go along with it until I see something to contradict it, and then I'll re-evaluate. If something that I believe to be true is proven wrong then I'll immediately concede the facts and change my position. I'll admit to my ignorance, learn something from it and move forward. Ego isn't a factor for me; true and correct information is the top priority. But that's not typical in this country, the exact opposite is! People don't do what I do. They avoid, deny, argue and ridicule! And if the truth bothers people so much, they must be in some sort of state of hypnosis. That much is clear. When I make a true, correct and factual statement and then I get the vast majority of people taking issue with me, then something is clearly wrong in this society. Americans are brainwashed. Why would they so willingly engage in arguing against scientifically validated facts? Are they mind controlled?[6] I once had someone argue with me about

---

[5] *Change Your Thoughts, Change Your Life: Living the Wisdom of the Tao* by Dr. Wayne W. Dyer

[6] https://en.wikipedia.org/wiki/Project_MKUltra

some declassified FBI documents that I showed him straight from the FBI's website (I'll show you soon). He told me that "those are fake documents." Oh, but they were on the FBI's web archive! He just didn't like the contents! Why would people be so irrational? People are always doing that, it's only one example of thousands that I encounter daily on social media. People are absolutely hypnotized. No doubt about that. The fact is that the government engages in mind-control all the time, working to pull the wool over your eyes and keep you from seeing the truth. They put out misinformation everywhere, in many different formats, and they work to keep you drugged up as much as possible. But guess what? They keep the truth hidden right before your very eyes. Pay very close attention and use your logic skills, this is very important! Intelligent people engage in open minded research, investigate the facts, verify them, and once verified, accept them as true! Does that make sense to you? 2+2=4 always and forever, concrete facts never change. So get used to that idea while we proceed into this presentation. Again, this is a logic-based presentation. Please pay attention and drop your biases. If you want to learn anything here an open mind is required. As long as you're open-minded and willing to learn you're OK. You don't have to know everything. Unless you're one who argues with verified facts (the vast majority are guilty, I'm very sorry to say) then you're open minded enough to proceed. Being open minded is apparently impossible for most people and I don't understand that concept. I've always been a very open-minded person. I question everything that there is to question. I'm that rare breed that common people can't stand. And I'm proud to be one thanks! And I'm not mind-controlled because of it! I found out the truth. Not very many people do! But you can if you pay close attention! Logic says to pay attention to what's going on. It's advantageous to know about the wicked world that we live in, it's a positive thing. It's called protecting yourself from harm by staying informed. People don't seem to understand that ignorance will get them six feet under, being informed is common sense. There's no reason not to be informed. People are very naive for trusting this place. A wise policy in the land of capitalism would be to trust nobody out in society and always double check things. Never, ever trust anybody for any information, always get it yourself. Look it up and research it yourself and find out for yourself. If you don't do your own research, you'll end up being lied to and very possibly dead if you're sitting in one of those fake doctor offices. Never trust them, always only rely upon yourself. Don't trust me either! Check my facts and look yourself! Don't take my word on anything! Double-check the links, cross-reference and verify it all! Trusting people in this society isn't possible with all the brainwashed Americans walking around and all of the sleazy corruption that causes the government and its institutions to lie like bandits in an effort to maximize profits and keep people misinformed among other reasons. But don't worry about it, go ahead and walk around trusting this evil society, being naive, blindly trusting the system like fools. Allow them to destroy your life and the life of your children because of your ignorance. You'll end up six feet under, dead in a box if you're not paying attention in this society. You will quite literally die at the hands of the state if you're not careful.

Plato's *Allegory of the Cave* in depicts common humans as being chained in a cave, facing a wall of shadows with only a fire behind them. They perceive the world by watching the shadows on the wall. They sit in darkness with the false light of the fire behind them and fail to realize that this existence is, illusory and deceptive. They accept it as absolute reality because they know no other way, it is all they know. Plato then shows what might happen if the chained men were suddenly released from their bondage and let out into the real world. He describes how some people would immediately be frightened and want to return to the cave and their familiar dark existence, their comfort zone. Others would have more courage, look at the sun and finally see the world as it truly is, hence becoming enlightened or aware of the light of truth. They would then know that their previous existence was a lie, a mere shadow of the truth, and they would come to the understanding that their previous lives had been one of deception and have a far better understanding of the world around them. They would also want to help those still in the bondage of the cave to free themselves, only to find that many people would refuse to leave. They would also find that many of those fearful people were laughing at their enlightened state as if they were insane. Many would refuse to acknowledge any truth beyond their current existence in the cave simply because the truth is too overwhelming for them to face. If you take a look at the first *The Matrix* film, you will see a new interpretation or more modern presentation of this classic piece by Plato; the scene when Neo's mind is freed for example, and how overwhelmed he was, and how he had a severe panic attack upon his leaving the cave makes the point clear. People are conditioned like robots and deprogramming their minds brings about much anxiety and discomfort. That kind of a reaction is what holds most people in a state of denial. They'll have the truth sitting right in front of them, but they won't respond, they'll keep arguing and denying the reality of what they're being presented with. They're afraid of the unknown and they're afraid of knowing the truth about the world around them. But why should anyone be fearful of the truth?

Where were we? Oh yes; go ahead and take some of those drugs that they're passing out these days without researching the side effects, and have a good time with that. I don't care what the fake doctors say, you're the one who gets to die, so I think you'd better check it out! If you don't, and you end up with serious side effects, who's to blame? Who didn't check it out first? Who blindly said "Oh, OK doc, sure no problem!" upon being prescribed that drug? It's not the doctor's fault as much as it is your own, who's the one putting it in your mouth and swallowing? People don't seem to notice that this society isn't any different than Nazi Germany, and when you try to tell them that they make mockery and laugh like fools because they're brainwashed and brain-dead just like the Germans were. Did you ever notice that you're not allowed to leave without their permission? First you have to give them your hard-earned money, and then you have to carry a passport. We're locked in. It's a prison. And all the passports now have microchips for tracking your every movement.[7] Why is their permission required to travel about the world? What's the problem there? And when we leave, they track our every movement all over the world with chips. Hmm. Why? Tyranny is in place, chemicals are in our food, air and water, the lives of our brand new children are destroyed with vaccines[8] and drugs like Ritalin, which is admitted by the Drug Enforcement Agency (DEA) to be basically the same thing as cocaine[9], and

---

[7] http://www.pcworld.com/article/123246/article.html

[8] http://articles.mercola.com/sites/articles/archive/2011/05/30/in-memoriam-infant-deaths-and-vaccination.aspx

[9] https://www.dea.gov/taxonomy/term/346

studies show that it's actually more potent than cocaine[10]. Nice medicine for young developing minds huh? Brains that aren't fully developed yet being prescribed with something like Ritalin isn't too bright of an idea. I challenge people to prove the DEA wrong in what they say about Ritalin. If they argue and give their kids Ritalin anyway, whose fault was it when they die later in life of drug addiction?

Ritalin – Cocaine Comparison
U.S. Department of Justice Drug Enforcement Agency (DEA) Drug and Chemical Evaluation Section for Methylphenidate (Ritalin®)

<u>Overview and Key Findings</u>

1. Ritalin is a Schedule II stimulate, structurally and pharmacologically similar to amphetamines and cocaine and has the same dependency profile of cocaine and other stimulants.

2. Ritalin produces amphetamine and cocaine-like reinforcing effects including increased rate of euphoria and drug liking. Treatment with Ritalin in childhood predisposes takers to cocaine's reinforcing effects.

3. In humans, chronic administration of Ritalin produced tolerance and showed cross-tolerance with cocaine and amphetamines.

4. Ritalin is chosen over cocaine in self-administered preference studies in non-human primates.

5. Ritalin produces behavioral, physiological and reinforcing effects similar to amphetamines.

6. Ritalin substitutes for cocaine and amphetamines in scientific studies.

7. Children medicated with Ritalin who tried cocaine reported higher levels of drug dependence than those who had not used Ritalin.

8. Ritalin abuse is neither benign or rare in occurrence and is accurately described as producing severe dependence. Sweden removed Ritalin from its market in 1968 because of widespread abuse.

9. More high school seniors were abusing Ritalin than those taking it medically prescribed.

Side-effects of Ritalin: increased blood pressure, heart rate, respirations and temperature; appetite suppression, weight loss, growth retardation; facial tics, muscle twitching, central nervous system stimulation, euphoria, nervousness, irritability and agitation, psychotic episodes, violent behavior, paranoid

---

[10] http://articles.mercola.com/sites/articles/archive/2014/05/01/antidepressants-adhd-drugs.aspx

delusions, hallucinations, bizarre behaviors, heart arrhythmias, palpitations and high blood pressure; tolerance and psychological dependence and death

10. Ritalin will affect normal children and adults the same as those with attention and behavior problems. Effectiveness of Ritalin is not diagnostic.

CHADD, non-profit organization, which promotes the use of Ritalin, also receives a great deal of money from the drug manufacturer of Ritalin. CHADD does not inform its members of the abuse problems of Ritalin. CHADD portrays the drug as a benign, mild stimulant that is not associated with abuse or serious side-effects. Statements by CHADD are inconsistent with scientific literature.

11. The International Narcotics Control Board expressed concern that CHADD is actively lobbying for the use of Ritalin in children.

12. Ritalin is one of the top ten drugs involved in drug thefts and is being abused by health professionals as well as street addicts.

Note from Dr. Block: Since Adderall and Dexadrine are amphetamines, the above statements would also be true of them.

What's wrong with the American people allowing this to continue? They mindlessly submit their children to the state's so-called doctors like robots. They don't do any research on Ritalin, vaccines or anything else, and then they just hand over their kids. I feel really sorry for the children of America with their typical American parents mindlessly following the system while they end up addicted to Ritalin before their minds have even had time to develop yet, and with autism, sudden death, leukemia, etc. from their vaccines. When will they learn? These are brand new people here. They just came to this planet and they haven't had time to hurt anybody yet, but the American people are allowing them to be poisoned to death by the state with their vaccines. What the hell are you Americans doing? Question; if vaccines are safe, then what's this all about?

> "The Health Resources & Services Administration just released new dollar figures reflecting payouts from the National Vaccine Injury Compensation Program. The payouts for vaccine injuries just went past the whopping $4 billion mark. Using the government's own conclusion that only 1% of all vaccine injuries are reported, the $4 billion is just the tip of the iceberg. Despite assurances from CDC and our Federal agencies that all vaccines are safe, the payouts say otherwise."[11]

That is a very tightly controlled compensation program and it's really,

---

[11] https://childrenshealthdefense.org/news/4-billion-and-growing-u-s-payouts-for-vaccine-injuries-and-deaths-keep-climbing/

https://www.hrsa.gov/vaccine-compensation/data/index.html

really difficult to win a case. Most parents don't even try to go through the proceedings because it's so time consuming and full of hoops to jump through. These stats only reflect reported cases that have gone through the system and been paid out, they don't represent actual numbers of injuries. Those numbers have gone through the roof in the last decade. They're intentionally giving children cancer in their vaccines and naturopathic doctors are being murdered for blowing the whistle on *unlisted ingredients*:

> "A wave of mysterious deaths continues to plague practitioners in the field of holistic medicine, including chiropractors, herbalists and other alternative healers. Some of the deaths have been tied to research involving nagalase, an enzyme/protein made by cancer cells and viruses that cause immunodeficiency syndromes and autism. Renowned autism specialist, Dr. James Jeffrey Bradstreet, was researching the enzyme prior to his death in July 2015. His body was discovered floating in a North Carolina river with a single gunshot wound to the chest."[12]

Meanwhile cancer cures are hidden away from the public,[13] most people are put on unnecessary drugs by the state's doctors, apathy is pervasive, and nobody gives a shit because the people are, as the late great Jim Marrs[14] said, "all zombies." Even airline pilots are now permitted to fly while under the influence of Prozac and other mind-altering drugs with terrible side effects including suicidal thoughts, and nobody bats an eye[15]. Excuse me, but if I'm flying, I don't want a pilot on Prozac.

> "Depressed people who take medication such as Prozac to control their condition have a significantly impaired ability to drive, a study has claimed. 'Individuals taking antidepressants should be aware of the possible cognitive effects as [they] may affect performance in social academic and work settings,' wrote researchers."[16]

---

[12] http://www.naturalnews.com/055347_vaccines_dead_doctors_cancer_enzymes.html

[13] www.thetruthaboutcancer.com

[14] One of my favorite authors recently passed away. I give him much respect for his work. Thank you very much sir!

[15] http://www.nydailynews.com/news/money/pilots-prozac-finally-permitted-fly-regulators-drop-ban-article-1.165005

[16] http://www.telegraph.co.uk/news/2575396/Antidepressants-impair-driving-ability-in-the-depressed.html

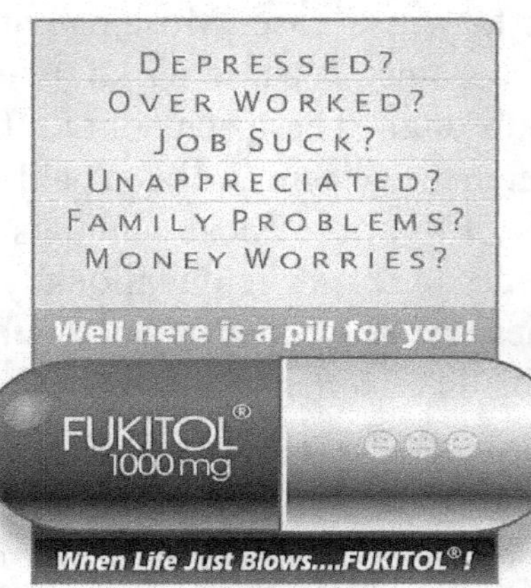

Problems? Here! Swallow this pill! The answer is in a bottle of toxic chemicals! All of your problems will be solved immediately! Only $129.99 per bottle while supplies last! Hurry, the big sale ends Friday! No prescription required!

Sadly enough, you can take Prozac and drive, but if you don't buckle your seat-belt you'll get pulled over, harassed and have money stolen from you by the state for making a freewill choice with your own body in the privacy of your own vehicle, meanwhile drivers on Prozac (and other dangerous drugs) engaged in reckless endangerment of other citizens are passing by on the freeway while the cop writes you your no seat-belt ticket.

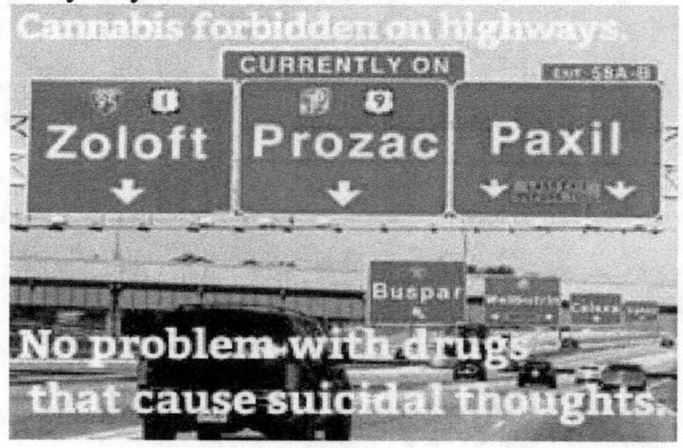

As a smoker of cannabis for decades I can attest to the fact that it provides what I term a tunnel vision type of focus. It helps the person settle down and focus on the activity at hand, which makes them better at just about every activity, including driving! As a matter of fact, many scientific studies conclusively prove that it has the very same effect for children with behavioral problems such as

ADD/ADHD, cannabis calms them down and provides focus![17]

> "Almost universally ADHD patients who therapeutically used cannabis reported it helped them pay attention in lecture, focus their attention instead of thinking of several ideas almost at the same time, helped them to stay on task and do their homework."
> **- David Bearman, MD**[18]

And no, I don't suggest that inexperienced users should smoke and drive. Studies show that inexperienced users, or first-time users, could be temporarily disoriented until they adapt to the effects of cannabis. After you've gained some experience and familiarity with the effects it's generally easy to adapt to and actually helps you focus and concentrate better unlike alcohol or Prozac. If you wanted a fair assessment on cannabis and driving, you've just seen it. You've also seen a fair assessment for Prozac and driving. Cannabis is the clear-cut winner. But they don't worry about weird drugs like Prozac they just tell us to buckle up!

> **Prozac** on freeways deemed safe (which creates dangerous freeways for innocent bystanders and everyone in general). **Permitted** by law.

> **No seat-belt** deemed unsafe. Immediate fines and penalties (never mind that it hurts nobody else). **Prohibited** by law.

Here's an idea; let's have grown adults make their own damn decision regarding their seat-belts and let's just say no to Prozac on our freeways! How about that? It seems to me that the police should be protecting and serving, not stealing our money and enforcing hypocritical laws. The standard reply among Americans is:

> "Well stop breaking the law and wear your seat-belt then, if you don't want to be ticketed."

They're simply not too bright. I personally do wear my seat-belt (for my own reasons not because of their law!), but that's not the point here. The point is that it's my choice! Or should be if it's truly a free country, which obviously it's not. Americans don't seem to get the point that the law is tyrannical, designed for two main reasons; 1) Extracting money from the populace and 2) Having a manufactured reason to pull people over. Among other reasons. And did you notice that busloads of children aren't required to wear seat-

---

[17] https://www.usatoday.com/story/news/world/2017/04/25/marijuana-pot-treatment-children-autism-cannabis-oil/100381156/

[18] https://unitedpatientsgroup.com/blog/2015/09/24/could-cannabis-be-a-safer-alternative-to-adhd-drugs

belts? Did you ever notice that glaring contradiction?

> **Large numbers of children** without seat-belts on school buses. No problem! Carry on about your day! **Permitted by law**.

> **Grown adults** in the privacy of their own vehicles without seat-belts. Immediate penalties and fines. **Prohibited by law**.

Aren't children the people who need protection the most? I'd say that if there's a seat-belt law, it should be for them, not for me. I think I can handle my own seat-belt just fine, thank you very much, but these children just might need some assistance! What happened to their theory of protecting the public by forcing them to wear seat-belts? It doesn't matter with little children on school buses? If we're going to protect the public with then let's try to be consistent about it! The current system isn't logical. Any and all laws that remove personal decision making from the equation are tyrannical laws: My definition of personal decision making is this; any decision that you make that only affects you directly. You're not hurting anyone else by choosing not to buckle up. That's your business, nobody else's. Who does it affect other than yourself possibly? Nobody. That's called making a personal decision. This is supposed to be a free country. If I'm alone in my home or in my vehicle, hurting nobody, then whose business is it but mine? Why should the police have the right to step in when I've not hurt or bothered anyone else, reprimand me and ticket me for making a private decision with my own body in the privacy of my own vehicle? Did I hurt somebody else when I did that, yes or no? Or was that just my own personal private decision? People need to wake up and realize that if there's no victim, there's no crime!

The 4th Amendment

The right of the people to be secure in their persons, houses, papers, and effects, against unreasonable searches and seizures, shall not be violated, and no Warrants shall issue, but upon probable cause, supported by Oath or affirmation, and particularly describing the place to be searched, and the persons or things to be seized.

With no reasonable suspicion of a crime or evidence of a crime committed, nobody has the right to search the contents of your car, home, office, body (person), etc. under any circumstances whatsoever without probable cause as described in the Constitution. Any search for any other reason is a direct violation of the 4th Amendment! Yes, "urinalysis for employment purposes" included.

Notice how it says "secure in their persons" first! The top priority is your body and your life! They use invasive laws to override the Constitution. Their seat-belt law gives them a manufactured excuse to invade the privacy and space of innocent bystanders who harm nobody else. Their law was broken and so now you are subject to their harassment and theft of your hard-earned money for making a personal decision in the privacy of your own rig! When it comes to mandatory urine testing for employment purposes, that constitutes an illegal search of your person. If you try to defend yourself by saying that it's an unconstitutional search, you'll either be out of a job or denied being hired, yet they have no problem with employees chugging Budweiser and drinking hard liquor.

"Well Bob, as long as the job gets done we're not concerned with your alcoholism or the fact that you get shitfaced and beat your wife every weekend, we'll still promote you and give you plenty of raises. Just don't smoke weed or let us hear about that, OK? We'd have to terminate you immediately for that as it's a direct violation of company policies."

Let's say that you're applying for a job, and during the hiring process there's a form for you to sign that says before you're eligible for hire the hiring manager has to come to your home and search every inch of your living space. After that he has to search your car. If you don't agree to that then you can't get a job. How would you like that? Well, UA is the same thing. Why do you allow that to happen? Americans just roll over and comply without a second thought. Mandatory urine testing for employment purposes is a totalitarian invasion of personal privacy. Do you want to look in the private contents of my body? Well, get a search warrant first as the constitution demands! Some would argue that it's necessary for public safety in situations such as airline pilots, but I already pointed out that Prozac is permitted for airline pilots! I've also demonstrated scientifically how very dangerous it is to take Prozac and drive, therefore urine testing is not about public safety! What's the excuse now? I think I just check-mated your theory that it's OK to invade the privacy of Americans! It's all about being dictators and targeting cannabis patients and users! Even people who are prescribed cannabis by their doctors in states where cannabis is supposedly legal are still getting fired from their jobs for having THC in their urine! Even people who live in states where cannabis is supposedly legal have to pass a urine test and if THC shows up, they're ineligible for hire! They can be raging alcoholics and get a job/keep a job, but if a doctor prescribes them with cannabis they get terminated and/or denied employment immediately! I'm so happy that cannabis is "legal" now in my home state! It's legal to purchase, it's just not legal to smoke! I personally will not submit for employment with companies who demand to see the contents of my bodily fluids, nor will I let them tell me that I have to vaccinate myself with toxic poison. Can I do the work effectively? Well then, I don't think you have a valid reason to go prying into the private contents of my body and you certainly have no right to tell me what to put into my body either! That's nobody's business but mine! If the job function is performed well then that's all that matters. Employers have the right to make sure you're doing the work properly, not to dictate your private lives! Forced vaccination is basically the boss attacking the employee with deadly biological weapons. And nobody can tell me that I'm exaggerating by calling them deadly biological weapons when vaccines are in fact known to cause paralysis, sudden death, and other fun things, not only in children but in adults too![19] You cannot force me to put something into my body that has been proven to kill people. I don't want your stinkin' job!

Also, did you notice that you have to have a license to do anything anymore? The government making unconstitutional laws for the purpose of extracting my money is fascism. Did you buy your

---

[19] vaxtruth.org/2015/01/flu-shot-kills

Fecal Excrement & Bodily Fluid Disposal[20] license yet? $18.00 at DSHS. What a bargain. Don't worry, they'll only fine you or imprison you if you refuse to purchase one. Don't you dare get caught shitting without a license! Unlawful urinating is a $47.00 fine. Excrement disposal costs run a bit higher; the penalty there is $110.00. And don't worry about the 90-year-old man who got put in jail and fined for feeding the homeless[21], or the people who get put in jail for collecting rain water on their own property.[22] White males dressed in dark sunglasses with white shirts and ties go onto people's private property and harass them, threatening to evict them from their own land for living off the grid without the government's unnecessary electricity.[23] Either give the government money, or get off of the land that they legally purchased, never mind that they're hurting nobody else.

> "We live in a completely corrupted world where every government is just a bunch of businessmen working for a bunch of bigger businessmen and none of them give a shit about the people." - **Woody Harrelson**

What were they doing that deserved jail time? What did they do to deserve being bothered by anyone at all? Did they deserve to be harassed like this just for using their own method of electricity? Liberty means that as long as you're not victimizing anyone else or trampling on anyone's rights, then you're innocent of all charges. If you're not bothering anyone else, then carry on and have a good time. Enjoy your freedom. The only true crime is victimizing other people. Nothing else. Can any of my readers name a true crime that doesn't involve a victim? Is there any such thing? There shouldn't be, not in the land of the free. Honestly, name one situation where it's appropriate to lock someone up or ticket someone for hurting nobody. Go ahead, give it your best shot. Tell me when it's appropriate to do that. That isn't freedom. That's fascism.

> "The Great Lie is that this is civilization. It's not civilized. It has literally been the most blood thirsty brutalizing system ever imposed upon this planet. This is not civilization, this is the Great Lie. Or if it does represent civilization, and that is truly what civilization is, then the Great Lie is that civilization is good for us." - **John Trudell**

---

[20] This is clever nonsense that I invented to make my point.

[21] http://www.nydailynews.com/news/national/man-90-arrested-week-feeding-homeless-article-1.2002790

[22] http://www.foxnews.com/real-estate/2012/08/16/man-jailed-for-collecting-rainwater-in-illegal-reservoirs-on-his-property.html

[23] https://thehomestead.guru/off-grid-home-condemned

Did you ever notice how thuggish the cops are these days and how they all look like terrorists in the military now instead of plain blue like the good old days? What happened to Barney Fife? I don't like seeing cops that look like terrorists. They don't necessarily make me feel safe.

And did you hear that in order to be a cop now you have to be a moron? They have to score dumb on an IQ test.[24] Yeah, that's right, if they score too high on an IQ test, they can't join the team. Not everywhere but it's becoming more and more common now for that to be the case. They don't want intelligent cops that can figure out that they're being told to enforce tyrannical laws, they want dumb thug types that will do anything they say. They want young, dumb, gung-ho punks for cops to enforce their tyranny without giving them any back talk, just "doing their jobs" as instructed without questioning anything they're told to do. They make laws to force people to hand over their hard-earned money and if we don't pay, we get thrown in jail and given tickets. You're given two choices; 1) Fork over your money to the government or 2) Fork over your money to the government. Either purchase their license (1) or get fined (2) for not purchasing. It's a con job. It's rigged in their favor, which is the definition of tyranny. But don't worry about that Americans, I think *American Idol* is on! Hurry, you'll miss your show! Don't forget to keep your shitting license up to date, don't let it expire, they'll fine you for that too ($47.00).

---

[24] http://abcnews.go.com/US/court-oks-barring-high-iqs-cops/story?id=95836

America has only 4.5% of the world's people, but they have 25% of the world's prisoners.[25] It's so nice living in a free country. The vast majority of those prisoners are non-violent drug offenders. Cannabis users cover a very high percentage. Who honestly feels that smoking a plant that has never killed anyone, ever, deserves jail time or a ticket? Seriously? Under-aged children are permitted to walk into *WalMart* and purchase aspirin, Tylenol and other toxic and deadly chemical drugs right over the counter with no ID or age restrictions whatsoever.[26] Any 9-year-old is allowed to do that! Those under-aged children can then take those deadly drugs out of the store and do whatever they please with them. I don't see anyone picketing in the street out in front of *WalMart*, complaining about under-aged children having access to deadly chemicals, and I don't see anyone worried or concerned about feeding their children toxic *McDonald's* food[27] but I see people complaining about cannabis.

> **Deadly chemicals** from *WalMart* and *McDonald's*, proven to cause cancers and kill people **APPROVED** for their children, considered normal and acceptable.

> **Therapeutic herbs** never proven to have killed anyone, **hundreds of studies show that it cures cancers**[28] **NOT APPROVED!** Demonized and considered inappropriate for their children; totally and completely unacceptable.

Start paying better attention people! Your society is a fraud! The drug war is a fraud, the government puts those drugs out there in the first place.[29] Wake up Americans your government are criminals. They are actively engaged in the trampling of our rights to be free and live the way we want to live as sovereign citizens when they ticket us for making a personal decision while hurting nobody else, and that goes for everything, not just their ridiculous seat-belt law.

In nursing homes, they totally cut off all food and all water and just let the patient suffer to death. I know because I worked in those homes. But to this very day only five states are allowing for physician assisted suicide. Why would cutting off someone's food

---

[25] *American Civil Liberties Union* (ACLU) statistics

[26] Call them up and ask them! I did! It's true!

[27] http://www.top10grocerysecrets.com/2015-07-02-top-10-toxic-ingredients-used-mcdonalds.html

[28] https://scholar.google.com/scholar?hl=en&as_sdt=0%2C48&q=cannabinoids+cancer&oq=

[29] https://www.thenewamerican.com/world-news/north-america/item/17396-u-s-government-and-top-mexican-drug-cartel-exposed-as-partners

and water and letting them dehydrate and starve to death be OK, but putting them out of their misery really quick is illegal in 45 states? Just an observation. Apparently suffering is what we're supposed to do if we're terminally ill, and the state has more rights to our own bodies than we do. That's what they think, anyway. Forcing people with toxic poison and calling it medicine, destroying their lives then making them suffer to death when they're in nursing homes at the end of their lives isn't freedom, it's tyranny. My body is my choice, I'll not have anyone step in and tell me otherwise. I won't comply. I won't allow my body to be regulated by the state, that's out of their jurisdiction. It's my choice, not theirs. If I want to shoot heroin in private, that's my option. It's my life. Nobody owns my body but me. They'd have no problem selling me chemotherapy and destroying my life that way if I were ever to be diagnosed with cancer due to all of the chemicals and poisons that the FDA approves for my food, water and so-called medicine. Americans have permission to poison themselves with society's poisons but for some reason illegal drugs aren't allowed. Go figure. Chemotherapy is a derivative of nitrogen mustard gas from WWII. [30] It's as toxic as toxic gets. It kills everything it touches. Nurses wear special protective clothing when they handle it. Some of them end up getting cancer from handling it for so many years on the job![31] But they call that medicine and they have absolutely no problem whatsoever selling it to me, as long as I can pay. If anyone has a list of people successfully cured with this stuff, I'd like to see it! In the case of Lance Armstrong, the bicyclist, he had a form of testicular cancer that is typically much easier to cure and as a result they were able to kill the cancer off with chemo before they killed Lance, but cases like that are extremely rare! Nearly unheard of. Of course, they had a media frenzy over it and misinformed the public, trying to make chemo look good because of their poster boy Lance Armstrong's success with it. It's bullshit.

"Most cancer patients in this country die from chemotherapy." - **Dr. Allen Levin**

Chemotherapy works such great wonders on cancer that Ronald Reagan secretly went to Germany in 1985 and consulted Hans Nieper, M.D. and had Carnivora, a pure extract of the Venus

---

[30] https://en.wikipedia.org/wiki/Nitrogen_mustard

[31] http://scrubsmag.com/chemotherapy-drugs-are-killing-nurses/

Flytrap plant, as a treatment instead of chemotherapy. I find it amusing that the man sitting in the oval office rejected chemotherapy. As a matter of fact, before he went to Germany for Carnivora treatments he was receiving laetrile[32] treatments in the oval office for 13 months! Chemotherapy simply was not an option for Ronald Reagan! *PubMed*, which is a government sponsored website that specializes in the publishing of research studies, published a conclusive study on five-year survival rates for chemotherapy patients in both America and Australia and it shows that 98% of chemo recipients are dead within five years![33] Ronnie knew the real story apparently! And he didn't die from cancer! He lived 19 more years and died from something else. Did you notice that elites rarely or never die from cancer? Name a President of the USA who died of cancer. Name any world leader who did. Any billionaire. Any top CEO or lawmaker? Go ahead. Name one. Given that nitrogen mustard gas is nothing but a toxic poison that kills everything it touches, why would that surprise anyone? That's what poison does. The population gets poison so-called medicine while the elites secretly get real medicine that works like Laetrile and Carnivora.

> "We have a multi-billion-dollar industry that is killing people, right and left, just for financial gain. Their idea of research is to see whether two doses of this poison is better than three doses of that poison." - **Dr. Glenn Warner**

Yet people still submit themselves for chemotherapy. Are they brainwashed? Yes. If Ford Motors produced a car that fails to start 98% of the time, would it still be on the market? Chemo kills people 98% of the time, but it's still for sale! Who with any common sense believes that injecting nitrogen mustard gas into their veins will make it all better? So why volunteer for it then? They're mind-controlled slaves, blindly submitting themselves for extermination, that's precisely what they are.

---

[32] *World Without Cancer: The Story of Vitamin B17* by G. Edward Griffin

[33] https://www.ncbi.nlm.nih.gov/pubmed/10472327

"May I help you sir?

"Yes Ma'am. I was just diagnosed with cancer. I'm here to allow the government to poison my system with **nitrogen mustard gas** until I die a slow and painful death.

"Oh OK. **We'll be more than happy to poison you to death**, but first we need to **take your money**. Have a seat and we'll call your name soon to get your insurance and credit card information."

Why else would anyone submit to chemotherapy, if they're not brainwashed? Can anyone provide me with *scientific studies* to show that intravenous nitrogen mustard gas is a healthy option? Where's the evidence to support chemotherapy as a therapeutic substance as opposed to just toxic poison? The science dictates that it's toxic poison, period. So where is the logic in saying OK to chemotherapy?

"My studies have proved conclusively that untreated cancer victims live up to four times longer than treated individuals." - **Dr. Hardin B. Jones, PhD**

They'd put me six feet under just like they do everyone else with chemotherapy as long as I gave them a proper insurance card or a credit card to cover their bill. They'll give me drugs with no therapeutic value whatsoever as long as it makes them money. Why am I allowed to use deadly drugs that make them money, but I'm not allowed to use the ones that they can't profit from? The only reason I'm not allowed to shoot heroin legally is because the capitalist swine can't profit from it. Legally anyway. Your government keeps drugs like cocaine and heroin illegal because it gives them a good excuse to incarcerate poor black kids in lower income urban areas. Since Tricky Dicky Nixon launched the War on Drugs in the 1970s, incarceration rates have skyrocketed. This is officially the society with the highest rates of incarceration in the history of the world, and the vast majority of those incarcerated are there because they didn't hurt anyone else, they're non-violent drug offenders as well as being disproportionately black.

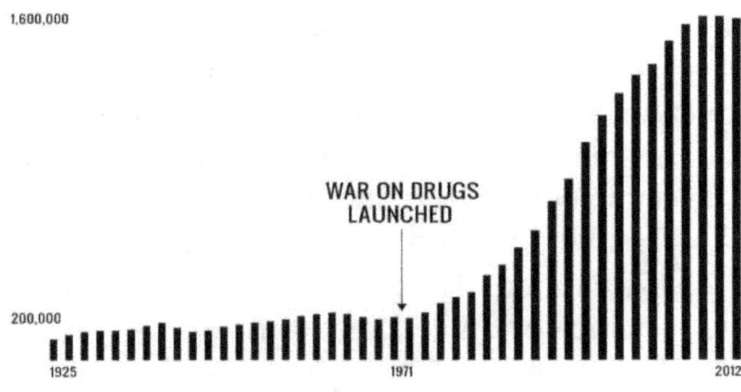

**THE U.S. STATE AND FEDERAL PRISON POPULATION
HAS INCREASED OVER 800% IN JUST 40 YEARS**

The troops in Afghanistan are guarding those poppy plants and heroin production has increased dramatically over there since the USA took over in 2001.[34] The troops tend the crops and then the CIA and other government importing agencies make the drop ship. Slick Willy and Daddy Bush used to bring cocaine into the Arkansas airport quite frequently. Millions of dollars worth at a time. There has even been a documentary film made about it to present the evidence and alert the public:

> "The Mena Connection establishes unequivocally that both Vice-president George H. W. Bush and Governor Bill Clinton had direct involvement in the CIA's cocaine smuggling operation at Arkansas' Mena Airport during the 1980s. Aircraft loaded with illegal weapons for the Contras in Honduras returned to Mena with tons of Columbia cocaine used to finance the operation. Reprising documentary evidence Reed presents in his 1994 bestselling book, Compromised: Clinton, Bush and the CIA , the film also establishes that Clinton also deliberately obstructed investigations into Mena by local and federal prosecutors and the IRS. Half the documentary is devoted to exposes a local Arkansas TV reporter and a WMAQ (Chicago) reporter did on cocaine smuggling at Mena during the congressional investigation into Iran Contra.* The other half consists of lengthy interviews with whistle blower Terry Reed and his wife Janis."[35]

The CIA (Cocaine Importing Agency) imports cocaine and heroin[36], dumps it out onto the streets and then the cops round people up and put them in jail for possession, that's why your jails are clogged up in this country. First, they put it there, and then they throw people in jail for having it. It's a con job and an excuse to incarcerate people, mostly lower income blacks. It's also a great

---

[34] https://www.rt.com/news/156128-afghanistan-drugs-usa-heroin/

[35] https://stuartjeannebramhall.com/2016/10/19/cia-cocaine-trafficking-bill-clinton-and-the-mena-airport/

[36] http://www.collective-evolution.com/2017/06/22/how-the-cia-operated-a-drug-smuggling-airline-for-heroin-the-911-connection

excuse to seize their assets, homes, cars, etc. and destroy their lives in order to bring the population down. The water in Detroit, MI is tainted with deadly toxins and contaminated with lead. Their infrastructure has been reduced to nearly third world status.[37] The schools are shutting down,[38] and Trump spends $16,000,000 to drop one single bomb ("Mother of All Bombs") on Afghanistan as well as 59 bombs at the cost of about $1,000,000 each on Syria, for a total of $75 million, while he ignores the tainted water in Flint, Detroit, Sacramento, CA,[39] and central Texas.[40]

The drug war is, by and large, a war on American ghettos. People who live in the ghetto are desperate and then here comes the cocaine courtesy of the CIA and it gives them a chance to make some money. Any fool can see that making money is a possibility in the cocaine business. In their desperation they do whatever it takes to survive. Try living poor in the ghetto sometime and then tell me that it wouldn't be tempting to make some quick money selling coke! Their other option is joining the military. They can turn into criminal gang members or they can join the military. Those are pretty much their options, and the government has it set up that way for a reason. That way they can either lock them up or they can use them for

---

[37] http://www.naturalnews.com/052739_toxic_chemicals_water_supply_Detroit_Michigan.html

[38] http://www.detroitnews.com/story/news/local/detroit-city/2016/04/14/detroit-schools-water-contamination-lead-copper/83048856/

[39] https://patch.com/california/pacificpalisades/californias-contaminated-tap-water-poses-cancer-risk-study

[40] http://www.khou.com/news/texas-drinking-water-makes-pipes-and-plumbing-radioactive_20160919032944620/320744548

cannon fodder. It's in the government's interest either way.

I find the way that the US government and the American citizens treat the returned troops repulsive! Many, if not most of our nation's homeless are veterans of the military. They sacrifice and go off to war and then they come home injured and psychologically disturbed and the government tells them to fuck off, go sleep in the gutter! That's not right! I support those troops as human beings! Shame on you US government for letting USA's veterans go homeless in the streets! And shame on typical Americans for sporting yellow ribbons and flags but never actually doing anything to help the returned troops!

"Military men are just dumb stupid animals, to be used as pawns in foreign policy."
- **Henry Kissinger**

Of course, sometimes those who are desperate in low income urban areas have above average intelligence. Sometimes they play it smart and create a rare third option for themselves; Instead of staying in a life of crime, they work the black market for a while and then use the money to go to one of society's institutions for that piece of paper called a degree. Some of them end up with decent jobs and lives. They found their ticket out of the ghetto thanks to the cocaine being dumped into their neighborhoods by the CIA.

"Charlie used to work after school,
At the cinema show,
Gotta hustle if he wants an education,
Yeah, he's got a long way to go.
Now he's out on the streets all day,
Selling crack to the people who pay.
Got an AK-47 for his best friend,
Business the American way."
- **Queensryche *Empire* (title track)**

They have liquor stores on every corner in places like Harlem and Detroit and a gun shop on every other corner. Not literally, but the point is clear. Again, they have it set up that way for a reason. They're making war on their own people. Prisons are making money hand over fist because it's a business, the more people they lock up the more they get paid! The prison industry in the USA is for profit! How wrong is that? Typical Americans don't mind that they lock people up just for the sake of making money in the land of the free. They don't mind at all.

"The two largest for-profit prison companies in the United States – GEO and Corrections Corporation of America – and their associates have funneled more than $10 million to candidates since 1989 and have spent nearly $25 million on lobbying efforts. Meanwhile, these private companies have seen their revenue and market share soar. They now rake in a combined $3.3 billion in annual revenue and the private federal prison population more than doubled between 2000 and 2010, according to a report by the Justice Policy Institute. Private companies house nearly half of the nation's immigrant detainees, compared to about 25 percent a decade ago, a Huffington Post report found. In total, there are now about 130 private prisons in the country with about 157,000 beds."[41]

These companies lobby to keep cannabis illegal so that they won't lose revenue. *Corrections Corporation of America* spends nearly $1,000,000 per year, they need to keep locking people up for smoking a therapeutic herb because it makes them money. They don't care about the science showing that it's the most powerful medicinal herb on the planet[42] and that it doesn't hurt or kill anyone,

---

[41] https://www.washingtonpost.com/posteverything/wp/2015/04/28/how-for-profit-prisons-have-become-the-biggest-lobby-no-one-is-talking-about/?utm_term=.b5e838feea55

[42] https://medicalmarijuana.procon.org/view.resource.php?resourceID=000884

all they care about are their precious profits. Locking people up for profit incentives; what a concept. Only in the good old USA, the land of the free.

The media is controlled. The press isn't free. Six corporations, all of whom have pretty much the same ownership at the top of the pyramid, own and control roughly 90% of all the news and information that you get to see and hear[43] in the mainstream. If you've ever seen the movie *V for Vendetta* our controlled press is very much the same. During the Bush administration it became public knowledge that the White House was feeding *FOX News* "talking points" for their broadcasts.[44] In plain English, it means that the White House was running the press. The USA has pretty much always had a controlled press.

> "Operation Mockingbird was a secret campaign by the United States Central Intelligence Agency (CIA) to influence media. Begun in the 1950s, it was initially organized by Cord Meyer and Allen W. Dulles, it was later led by Frank Wisner after Dulles became the head of the CIA. The organization **recruited leading American journalists into a network to help present the CIA's views**, and funded some student and cultural organizations, and magazines as fronts. As it developed, it also worked to influence foreign media and political campaigns, in addition to activities by other operating units of the CIA."[45](emphasis my own)

Typical Americans will see this information and say "well, that was a long time ago" and the only source they'll trust is *CNN* or some other official source.

> "We'll know that our disinformation program is complete when everything the American public believes is false." - **William Casey, CIA Director, 1981**

> "We are grateful to the *Washington Post, The New York Times, Time Magazine* and other great publications whose directors have **attended our meetings and respected their promises of discretion** for almost forty years. It would have been impossible for us to develop our plan for the world if we had been subjected to the lights of publicity during those years. But, the world is now more sophisticated and prepared to **march towards a world government**. The supranational sovereignty of an intellectual elite and world bankers is surely preferable to the national auto-determination practiced in past centuries."
> - **David Rockefeller, 1991** (emphasis my own)

True, correct and verified news from the internet such as *WikiLeaks* is termed "fake internet news" by brainwashed Americans. At last fact check, *WikiLeaks* had a 100% record for accuracy. They base their news on declassified documents.

---

[43] http://www.businessinsider.com/these-6-corporations-control-90-of-the-media-in-america-2012-6

[44] http://www.huffingtonpost.com/steve-young/scott-mcclellan-white-hou_b_115099.html

[45] http://www.theblackvault.com/documentarchive/operation-mockingbird/

I wish that I didn't have to tell you that your so-called news is jam packed full of blatant lies as well as nearly completely censored, but it's true. Do you remember the so-called news event that claimed that Osama bin Laden had been captured? Supposedly they buried him at sea. But there were no eyewitnesses, no pictures, no videos, no nothing, and the American public bought into it hook, line and sinker, celebrating in the streets like morons. Not only that, just about the entire Navy SEAL Team 6 that supposedly did the heroic capturing of Osama turned up dead in a mysterious and "coincidental" helicopter crash.[46] That's mighty convenient for the liars in the White house, huh? Try fact checking *FOX News* or *CNN* sometime and let's compare, shall we? I enjoyed the fake video that the CIA made of Osama bin Laden claiming responsibility for 911[47], didn't you? See the photo below, investigate the links and watch the *YouTube* video[48] on this topic.

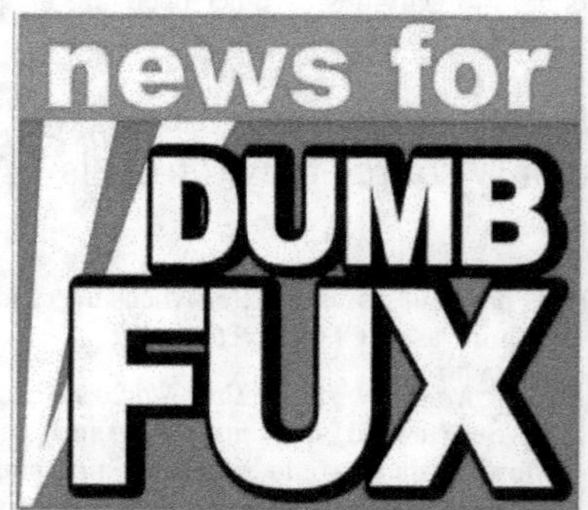

Check out the fat cheeks, the short, pudgy nose and the darker skin complexion on the confession video as compared to the authentic Osama on the right. This fraudulent CIA-made video aired on news networks worldwide!

And let's not forget that Osama was fully funded and trained up proper by the CIA themselves in Afghanistan during the Soviet Union's presence there in the 1980s.

---

[46] http://www.washingtontimes.com/news/2015/aug/5/obama-stonewalls-seal-team-6-extortion-17-helicopt/

[47] http://www.whatreallyhappened.com/WRHARTICLES/osamatape.html

[48] https://www.youtube.com/watch?v=1W6QLfXE3wA

> "Bin Laden was, though, a product of a monumental miscalculation by western security agencies. Throughout the 80s he was armed by the CIA and funded by the Saudis to wage jihad against the Russian occupation of Afghanistan."[49]

They created him just like they created Saddam Hussein, by arming him, funding him and offering full military training as well. So please, don't try to claim that your government is working to protect you from terrorists, because clearly that isn't the case at all! Al Qaeda and ISIS are CIA creations as well; trained, armed and funded by them too![50]

Your history books are fake too, by the way. You've been conned. You've been living in an experimental society your entire lives and you've been lied to about almost everything. You're in a giant military industrial prison complex somewhat similar to the movie *Escape from New York* only the size of a whole country and it has a police force inside. If you disobey the laws inside the giant prison, they send you to their smaller prisons so that capitalists can profit from your incarceration. Do you still believe you're free? We're nothing but a bunch of lab rats to them and they've been lying to us about everything! They're conducting experiments on us! Take a look around! When was the last time you saw this on *CNN*? The FBI reporting on Hitler's hideout in Argentina! Hitler was allowed to escape after the war.[51] The US government knew he escaped and left him alone. They likely set it up for him and helped him. 200 pages of FBI files prove this. I definitely claim this as evidence! There are over 200 pages because they knew where he was for decades. And they did nothing! Photographic evidence is seen below.

---

[49] https://newsone.com/1205745/cia-osama-bin-laden-al-qaeda/

[50] https://www.globalresearch.ca/america-created-al-qaeda-and-the-isis-terror-group/5402881

[51] *Hitler in Argentina: The Documented Truth of Hitler's Escape* by Harry Cooper

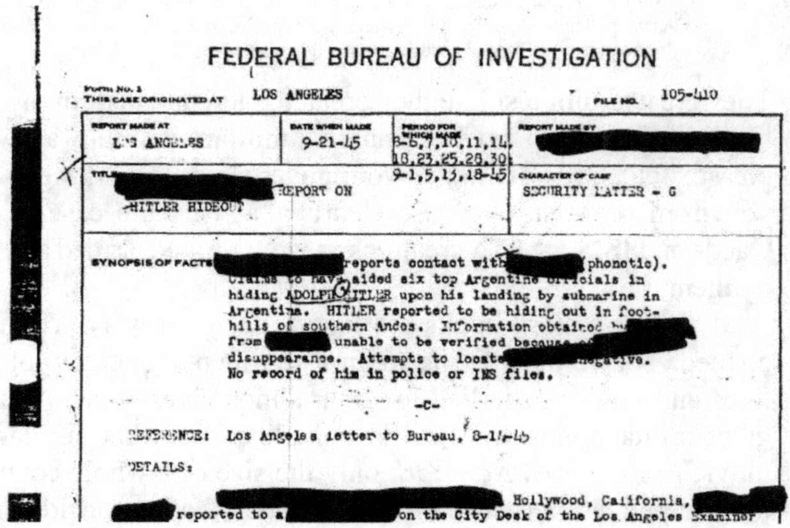

FEDERAL BUREAU OF INVESTIGATION

Straight from the FBI's very own website, there are over 200 pages of documents making it very hard to deny. On the first page you'll see that they had reports of him landing via submarine in Argentina, and then you'll see several subsequent reports indicating that he was allowed to live a life of luxury in Argentina, courtesy of the US government.[52]

Are you still asleep? Go look, it's on the FBI's page.[53] The photo above is an exact match. No photo editing tricks here. No tampering signs. This is a real image. I made it large so that you can compare the features. Every detail in the facial features checks out as the same person; same chin, same nose, same eyebrow ridges,

---

[52] https://vault.fbi.gov/adolf-hitler/adolf-hitler-part-01-of-04

[53] If by some chance it gets removed from the actual website of the FBI, I've downloaded the entire 200-page .pdf file myself and I'm sure that multiple websites will have them archived for download as well.

same ears, same facial shape, etc. It's the same man, just a little older with a little bit more fat on his face than before and/or his skin is looser, which is a normal sign of aging. Also take note that he's bald up top. The FBI files provide additional support making it absolutely undeniable. They keep things in plain view, but at the same time hidden! I showed this to an old high school friend of mine on *FaceBook* when I first discovered it, and he kept trying to defend the USA! He was a hippie type in high school, and now he's totally brainwashed, defending his totalitarian government like a good mind-controlled slave! What happened? I'm not sure. They might have taken his mind away by putting him on some drug maybe? He's not the same person that he was in high school, and that's a fact! His intelligence is gone, it's not there anymore, he's a moron now, but he used to be a bright, intelligent young man! There's only one kind of government that would allow Adolf Hitler to live in luxury after the war ended! This is indefensible! What kind of a person tries to keep defending the USA after they see this? A brainwashed one! Who wants to try and justify this to me? Why is it OK that your own government helped Hitler escape after the war, and why is it still a great country now that you've seen this information? This proves to me conclusively that the USA's government is far, far more criminal and far more dangerous than Adolf Hitler himself! He's supposed to be the biggest enemy of the world in the history of the world, isn't he? They aided and abetted Adolf Hitler and they've been playing mind games with you! They leave the truth out there for you to find! I found it! Now I'm showing it to you! You have always only seen the separate pieces of the puzzle, but you haven't tied them all together yet. I'm going to do that for you right now! Here's the rest! You can see all of this is true! Allow me to put this puzzle together for you, piece by piece. You've seen a little bit. There's much, much more! And don't forget to do cross reference checks and verify every last bit of this information yourself! **LOOK IT UP!! LOOK IT UP!! LOOK IT UP!! LOOK IT UP!! LOOK IT UP!!**

Take a look at this. They're engaged in mind-control against the population. They're conditioning our minds and brainwashing us with false information. Fake news, fake history, rigged elections, fake terrorist attacks, fake school shootings, the whole nine yards. Look at this! It's in plain view for all to see. They planned Trump's election long ago, see? Look! It was on the Simpsons in the year

2000! They like to leave us clues and hints to see if we can figure out what's going on while they brainwash us all. Are you laughing? I hope not. This is an emergency! This is factually correct, it really was on the Simpsons in the year 2000.

"If predicting Trump's rise in 2015 was tough, imagine doing it in 2000. Sixteen years ago — almost to the day — The Simpsons did just that." **- Rolling Stone Magazine**[54]

Your entire society is a manufactured artificial society, an industrial military prison complex designed for very specific purposes by the Luciferian secret societies who created America, the *Freemasons* and *Bavarian Illuminati*. Dwight D. Eisenhower, loved by Americans, Ike tried to give you fair warning in his famous farewell address.

"In the counsels of Government, we must guard against the acquisition of unwarranted influence, whether sought or unsought, by the Military Industrial Complex. The potential for the disastrous rise of misplaced power exists, and will persist. We must never let the weight of this combination endanger our liberties or democratic processes. We should take nothing for granted. Only an alert and knowledgeable citizenry can compel the proper meshing of the huge industrial and military machinery of defense with our peaceful methods and goals so that security and liberty may prosper together."[55]

---

[54] http://www.rollingstone.com/tv/news/flashback-watch-the-simpsons-predict-president-trump-in-2000-20160317

[55] https://www.youtube.com/watch?v=8y06NSBBRtY

YOU ARE ALL MIND-CONTROLLED

SLAVES. Wake up! Wake up! Wake up!

One of very few American Presidents that I have any respect for, John F. Kennedy, was persistent in warning us as well, as a matter of fact he was working to help free us from tyranny and they killed him for it. Thanks for doing the right thing brother!

"The very word secrecy is repugnant in a free and open society and we are as a people inherently and historically opposed to secret societies, to secret oaths and secret proceedings. We decided long ago that the dangers of excessive and unwarranted concealment of pertinent facts far outweigh the dangers which are cited to justify it. Even today, there is little threat of opposing a secret society by imitating its arbitrary restrictions. Even today, there is little value in insuring the future of our nation if our traditions do not survive with it and there is great danger that an announced need for increased security will be seized upon by those anxious to expand its meaning to the very limits of official censorship and concealment - that I do not intend to allow to permit to the extent that it is in my control. **For we are opposed around the world by a monolithic and ruthless conspiracy that relies primarily on covert means for expanding its sphere of influence — on infiltration instead of invasion — on subversion instead of elections — on intimidation instead of free choice — on guerrillas by night instead of armies by day.** It is a system which has conscripted vast human and material resources into the building of a tightly-knit, highly efficient machine that combines military, diplomatic, intelligence, economic, scientific and political operations. Its preparations are concealed not published. Its mistakes are buried, not headlined. Its dissenters are silenced, not praised. No expenditure is questioned, no rumor is printed, no secret is revealed".[56](emphasis my own)

Not to mention Abe Lincoln; it seems he had our best interests in mind as well, and coincidentally he was assassinated for the same reason, trying to issue his own currency through the treasury just like JFK.

"I see in the near future a crisis approaching that unnerves me and causes me to tremble for the safety of my country. As a result of the war, corporations have been enthroned and an era of corruption in high places will follow, and the money power of the country will endeavor to prolong its reign by working upon the prejudices of the people until all the wealth is aggregated in a few hands, and the Republic is destroyed." - **Abraham Lincoln**

Abe issued new currency via the treasury and bypassed the central bank. JFK did the same. Those are the only two presidents ever to bypass the central bank; both got shot. Gee, what a coincidence! You've been had! And time is running out.

They're trying to start up WWIII. Technically it's already started. They faked the other two World Wars, they were all financed on all sides[57] by the exact same banking families! The same bankers

---

[56] https://www.youtube.com/watch?v=286m0ZiBEFo

[57] https://www.youtube.com/watch?v=dP2bSlgWZWA

who own the Federal Reserve (which is a private bank not a federal institution) and the IRS, also control the Vatican, the EU, UK, Israel and almost every other country!

"I sincerely believe that banking establishments are more dangerous than standing armies." - **Thomas Jefferson**[58]

Here is a list of the Rothschild owned Central Banks worldwide:

"Afghanistan: Bank of Afghanistan Albania: Bank of Albania Algeria: Bank of Algeria Argentina: Central Bank of Argentina Armenia: Central Bank of Armenia Aruba: Central Bank of Aruba Australia: Reserve Bank of Australia Austria: Austrian National Bank Azerbaijan: Central Bank of Azerbaijan Republic Bahamas: Central Bank of The Bahamas Bahrain: Central Bank of Bahrain Bangladesh: Bangladesh Bank Barbados: Central Bank of Barbados Belarus: National Bank of the Republic of Belarus Belgium: National Bank of Belgium Belize: Central Bank of Belize Benin: Central Bank of West African States (BCEAO) Bermuda: Bermuda Monetary Authority Bhutan: Royal Monetary Authority of Bhutan Bolivia: Central Bank of Bolivia Bosnia: Central Bank of Bosnia and Herzegovina Botswana: Bank of Botswana Brazil: Central Bank of Brazil Bulgaria: Bulgarian National Bank Burkina Faso: Central Bank of West African States (BCEAO) Burundi: Bank of the Republic of Burundi Cambodia: National Bank of Cambodia Came Roon: Bank of Central African States Canada: Bank of Canada – Banque du Canada Cayman Islands: Cayman Islands Monetary Authority Central African Republic: Bank of Central African States Chad: Bank of Central African States Chile: Central Bank of Chile China: The People's Bank of China Colombia: Bank of the Republic Comoros: Central Bank of Comoros Congo: Bank of Central African States Costa Rica: Central Bank of Costa Rica Côte d'Ivoire: Central Bank of West African States (BCEAO) Croatia: Croatian National Bank Cuba: Central Bank of Cuba Cyprus: Central Bank of Cyprus Czech Republic: Czech National Bank Denmark: National Bank of Denmark Dominican Republic: Central Bank of the Dominican Republic East Caribbean area: Eastern Caribbean Central Bank Ecuador: Central Bank of Ecuador Egypt: Central Bank of Egypt El Salvador: Central Reserve Bank of El Salvador Equatorial Guinea: Bank of Central African States Estonia: Bank of Estonia Ethiopia: National Bank of Ethiopia European Union: European Central Bank Fiji: Reserve Bank of Fiji Finland: Bank of Finland France: Bank of France Gabon: Bank of Central African States The Gambia: Central Bank of The Gambia Georgia: National Bank of Georgia Germany: Deutsche Bundesbank Ghana: Bank of Ghana Greece: Bank of Greece Guatemala: Bank of Guatemala Guinea Bissau: Central Bank of West African States (BCEAO) Guyana: Bank of Guyana Haiti: Central Bank of Haiti Honduras: Central Bank of Honduras Hong Kong: Hong Kong Monetary Authority Hungary: Magyar Nemzeti Bank Iceland: Central Bank of Iceland India: Reserve Bank of India Indonesia: Bank

---

[58] Thomas Jefferson, May 28th, 1816

Indonesia Iran: The Central Bank of the Islamic Republic of Iran Iraq: Central Bank of Iraq Ireland: Central Bank and Financial Services Authority of Ireland Israel: Bank of Israel Italy: Bank of Italy Jamaica: Bank of Jamaica Japan: Bank of Japan Jordan: Central Bank of Jordan Kazakhstan: National Bank of Kazakhstan Kenya: Central Bank of Kenya Korea: Bank of Korea Kuwait: Central Bank of Kuwait Kyrgyzstan: National Bank of the Kyrgyz Republic Latvia: Bank of Latvia Lebanon: Central Bank of Lebanon Lesotho: Central Bank of Lesotho Libya: Central Bank of Libya (Their most recent conquest) Uruguay: Central Bank of Uruguay Lithuania: Bank of Lithuania Luxembourg: Central Bank of Luxembourg Macao: Monetary Authority of Macao Macedonia: National Bank of the Republic of Macedonia Madagascar: Central Bank of Madagascar Malawi: Reserve Bank of Malawi Malaysia: Central Bank of Malaysia Mali: Central Bank of West African States (BCEAO) Malta: Central Bank of Malta Mauritius: Bank of Mauritius Mexico: Bank of Mexico Moldova: National Bank of Moldova Mongolia: Bank of Mongolia Montenegro: Central Bank of Montenegro Morocco: Bank of Morocco Mozambique: Bank of Mozambique Namibia: Bank of Namibia Nepal: Central Bank of Nepal Netherlands: Netherlands Bank Netherlands Antilles: Bank of the Netherlands Antilles New Zealand: Reserve Bank of New Zealand Nicaragua: Central Bank of Nicaragua Niger: Central Bank of West African States (BCEAO) Nigeria: Central Bank of Nigeria Norway: Central Bank of Norway Oman: Central Bank of Oman Pakistan: State Bank of Pakistan Papua New Guinea: Bank of Papua New Guinea Paraguay: Central Bank of Paraguay Peru: Central Reserve Bank of Peru Philip Pines: Bangko Sentral ng Pilipinas Poland: National Bank of Poland Portugal: Bank of Portugal Qatar: Qatar Central Bank Romania: National Bank of Romania Russia: Central Bank of Russia Rwanda: National Bank of Rwanda San Marino: Central Bank of the Republic of San Marino Samoa: Central Bank of Samoa Saudi Arabia: Saudi Arabian Monetary Agency Senegal: Central Bank of West African States (BCEAO) Serbia: National Bank of Serbia Seychelles: Central Bank of Seychelles Sierra Leone: Bank of Sierra Leone Singapore: Monetary Authority of Singapore Slovakia: National Bank of Slovakia Slovenia: Bank ofSlovenia Solomon Islands: Central Bank of Solomon Islands South Africa: South African Reserve Bank Spain: Bank of Spain Sri Lanka: Central Bank of Sri Lanka Sudan: Bank of Sudan Surinam: Central Bank of Suriname Swaziland: The Central Bank of Swaziland Sweden: Sveriges Riksbank Switzerland: Swiss National Bank Tajikistan: National Bank of Tajikistan Tanzania: Bank of Tanzania Thailand: Bank of Thailand Togo: Central Bank of West African States (BCEAO) Tonga: National Reserve Bank of Tonga Trinidad and Tobago: Central Bank of Trinidad and Tobago Tunisia: Central Bank of Tunisia Turkey: Central Bank of the Republic of Turkey Uganda: Bank of Uganda Ukraine: National Bank of Ukraine United Arab Emirates: Central Bank of United Arab Emirates United Kingdom: Bank of England United States: Federal Reserve, Federal Reserve Bank of New York Vanuatu: Reserve Bank of Vanuatu Venezuela: Central Bank of Venezuela Vietnam: The State Bank of Vietnam Yemen: Central Bank of Yemen Zambia: Bank of Zambia Zimbabwe: Reserve Bank of Zimbabwe The FED and the IRS Virtually unknown to the general public is the fact that the US Federal Reserve is a privately owned company, siting on its very own patch of land, immune to the US laws."[59]

<u>THEY OWN THE WHOLE WORLD!!!!!!!!!!!!!!!!</u>

"Give me control over a nation's currency, and I care not who makes its laws."
- Mayer Amschel Rothschild

They own it all, minus a few countries anyway (Iran, N. Korea, Cuba) and they financed Hitler's rise to power[60] through

---

[59] http://humansarefree.com/2013/11/complete-list-of-banks-ownedcontrolled.html

[60] *Wall Street and the Rise of Hitler: The Astonishing True Story of the American Financiers Who Bankrolled the Nazis* by Antony C. Sutton

American corporations such as IG Farben,[61] Dupont,[62] IBM,[63] Ford Motors[64] and many others. Ford built many of Hitler's tanks and rigs. German diplomats awarded Henry Ford their highest honor, the Grand Cross of the German Eagle medal in July 1938.[65] Prescott Bush, the father of George H.W. Bush and the grandfather of George W. Bush was heavily involved in profiting off of Hitler's rise to power.

"...the new documents, many of which were only declassified last year, show that even after America had entered the war and when there was already significant information about the Nazis' plans and policies, he worked for and profited from companies closely involved with the very German businesses that financed Hitler's rise to power. It has also been suggested that **the money he made from these dealings helped to establish the Bush family fortune** and set up its political dynasty."[66](emphasis my own)

---

[61] https://en.wikipedia.org/wiki/IG_Farben#World_War_II_overview

[62] http://www.globalresearch.ca/profits-ber-alles-american-corporations-and-hitler/4607

[63] https://en.wikipedia.org/wiki/IBM_and_the_Holocaust

[64] https://www.theguardian.com/world/1999/aug/20/julianborger1

[65] http://www.washingtonpost.com/wp-srv/national/daily/nov98/nazicars30.htm

[66] https://www.theguardian.com/world/2004/sep/25/usa.secondworldwar

THEY'RE SPRAYING US LIKE COCKROACHES!!

"This is genocide. This is poison. This is murder by the United Nations. This element within our society that is doing this must be stopped... I personally have observed the planes that were standing still in Nebraska – Lincoln, Nebraska – at the Air National Guard...somebody has to do something about it. Somebody in Congress has to step forward and stop it now." - **Ted Gunderson, FBI Chief**

"What follows is a fairly exhaustive list of symptoms associated with chemtrail spraying. Each symptom has been identified by various individuals who have clocked their occurrence with the onset of chemtrails being laid down over their homes or businesses. This list has been organized in a descending order, with the most commonly experienced symptoms at the top.

• Headache
• Brain fog
• Fatigue
• Low energy
• Compromised immunity
• Disorientation
• Difficulty paying attention and concentrating
• Sinusitis
• Skin discomfort/irritation
• Joint pain
• Muscle pain
• Asthmatic (Breathing difficulties)

---

[67] https://www.bibliotecapleyades.net/sociopolitica/esp_sociopol_rothschild04.htm

- Dizziness
- Insomnia
- Memory loss
- Eye problems (blurred or fuzzy vision)
- Nausea
- Liver problems
- Gallballder dysfunction
- Tinnitus (distant ringing in ears or high pitched sound after spraying)
- Neck pain
- Scratchy throat
- Allergy symptoms
- Hay fever out of season
- Flu-like symptoms
- Susceptibility to colds
- General weakness
- Anxiety
- Lightheaded or faint
- Depression
- Coughing
- Sneezing
- Shortness of breath
- Vertigo
- Anger/Rage/Frustration issues
- MORGELLONS disease

Each of these symptoms is a normal occurrence in areas around the world where chemtrails have become a fact of life. Therefore, the first question one should ask themselves is the extent to which the "Chemtrail Coverup" is taking place right above them. The following essay may assist in that determination."[68]

Over the years, people have tested what is left behind in these unsanctioned poisonings. They have found the following :

Barium
Aluminum
Radium
Lithium
Manganese
Bacteria
Viruses
Other unknown biological agents
Other heavy metals

Chemtrails started showing up in 1999 and have increased considerably in frequency, especially from 2014 to 2016. Many used to think that they were just conspiracy theories. Now, it's quite obvious that they are not. The real question is, what is their purpose and who authorized the human population to be sprayed with this stuff?

Interesting enough, the countries being sprayed are all NATO members and include...
United States
Canada
United Kingdom
France
Germany
Netherlands
Italy

---

[68] http://www.geoengineeringwatch.org/chemtrail-syndrome-a-global-pandemic-of-epic-proportions-2/

Sweden
Croatia
Australia
Mexico
New Zealand
Haiti[69]

Also, we're all being poisoned with nuclear radiation too, but do you ever hear about it in the press? When's the last time FOX News told you that we're in deep shit with this Fukushima thing?

"As Adams tells us in his video, the sustainability of all life throughout the Northern hemisphere is in danger and the entire MSM up until now has been in a complete blackout mode except for recent reports. Do CNN, MSNBC and the rest of them think that if they DON'T report upon Fukushima, what's happening to the fish and our oceans is 'fake news'? Do they think that because we can't actually SEE the radiation, it's not really there? The MSM's failure to report upon Fukushima may be the final straw that not only breaks the camel's back but puts that camel out of our misery."[70]

Do the American people have a right to know what's coming over here from Japan? You bet your ass they do. But are they ever informed of what's going on by the press? Not much. But don't worry, this is a free country, right? People who actually have the intelligence to step up and call bullshit are hated in this society.

"Wait a goddamn minute! 2 + 2 doesn't = 17! It equals 4!"

But hey, if something is true then it's true! There is something very wrong when the truth gets ignored and avoided. What's up with that? Why is the verified truth considered controversial? Any society that censors the truth and abuses people who tell the truth is clearly tyrannical. I personally don't believe in censoring information, especially if it's true, but the American people certainly do! What's wrong with them, censoring and denying relevant and true information? Are they on drugs? Wait, don't answer that, I already know what they're putting in the water. Go have yourself a nice tall glass of carcinogenic, mind-numbing fluoride courtesy of the FDA. Don't worry about the Harvard study proving that it reduces brain function causing lower IQ in children.[71]

---

[69] http://www.rife.bztronics.com/chemtrails/chemtrails-ingredients.html

[70] http://www.antinewsnetwork.com/media-can-no-longer-hide-truth-fukushima-entire-world-danger/

[71] http://www.huffingtonpost.com/dr-mercola/fluoride_b_2479833.html

"In point of fact, fluoride causes more human cancer death, and causes it faster than any other chemical... I know of absolutely no, and I mean absolutely no means of prevention that would save so many lives as simply to stop fluoridation, or don't start it where it is otherwise going to be started. There you might save 30,000 or 40,000 or 50,000 lives a year. Cancer lives." - **Dr. Dean Burke, PhD**

And by the way, Prozac is 94% fluoride,[72] nice huh? Prozac water is the norm in the land of the free. The forced drugging of the population, quite literally!

"In reality, the fluoride added to the public water supplies in the United States is not organic fluoride at all. It is in fact fluorosilicic acid, which is purchased in bulk from chemical companies, who must be laughing loudly at the idea that they can actually sell this toxic waste product. Why? Because if cities weren't buying it and putting it into the public water supply, these industrial companies would have to spend millions of dollars disposing of fluorosilicic acid because it is an EPA regulated toxic waste. Let me put this another way -- fluorosilicic acid is a toxic waste byproduct that is produced in the United States by various chemical companies. It represents such a health hazard to human beings that it is regulated by the EPA, and must be disposed of as a toxic waste. And yet, municipalities throughout the United States actually purchase this product and then drip it into the public water supply, and simultaneously call it 'fluoride.' Fluorosilicic acid is not fluoride, it is something very different, and it strikes me as downright bizarre that it is perfectly legal to dump this toxic waste product into the rivers and streams of America as long as it passes through the bodies of human beings first. In other words, it's illegal to take a bucket of fluorosilicic acid and dump it into a stream, but it is perfectly legal to dump it into the bodies of human beings, whose waste products will subsequently enter those same streams and rivers." - **Mike Adams,** *NaturalNews*

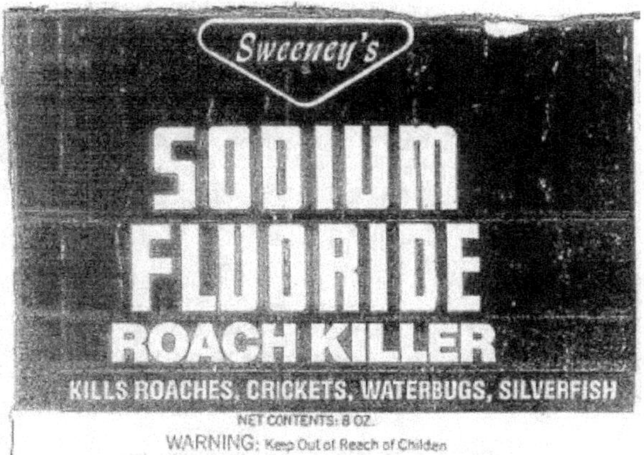

Come on down! You've just won a tall glass of roach killer! Don't forget to put lotsof ice into your glass! It goes down much smoother if it's ice cold!

"Let me get a sip of water here... you figure this stuff is safe to drink? Actually, I don't care, I drink it anyway. You know why? Because I'm an American and I expect a little cancer in my food and water. I'm a loyal American and I'm not happy unless I let government and industry poison me a little bit every day." - **George Carlin**

---

[72] https://www.youtube.com/watch?v=VTXS1nozFnQ

"As a research chemist of established standing, I built within the past 22 years, 3 American chemical plants and licensed 6 of my 53 patents. Based on my years of practical experience in the health-food and chemical field, let me warn: fluoridation of drinking water is criminal insanity, sure national suicide. Don't do it.... Even in smallquantities, sodium fluoride is a deadly poison to which no effective antidote has been found. Every exterminator knows that it is the most efficient rat-killer .... Sodium fluoride is entirely different from organic calcium fluoro-phosphate needed by our bodies and provided by nature."
- **Dr. E.H. Bronner, 1952**[73]

Now that I'm living a non-toxic lifestyle as much as possible (which is the only way to avoid becoming a victim of the state in this society), I can actually smell the chemicals in the public water supply when I pour a glass. To me, it smells like a swimming pool, whereas before, when I was a consumer of society's poisons, I couldn't smell it at all! I had been desensitized, and most of you are the same. It's there and it's as plain as day, but you can't tell, because to you it's normal. Try detoxing your body, and then smell your public water. You'll see. Hitler and the Nazis used fluoride to keep the population docile, comatose and easy to control. They're poisoning you and that's a proven fact. Is anybody home, McFly? Again, we're nothing but a bunch of lab rats to them!

"There will be, in the next generation or so, a pharmacological method of making people love their servitude, and producing dictatorship without tears, so to speak, producing a kind of painless concentration camp for entire societies, so that people will in fact have their liberties taken away from them, but will rather enjoy it, because they will be distracted from any desire to rebel by propaganda or brainwashing enhanced by pharmacological methods. And this seems to be the final revolution." - **Aldous Huxley**

<u>YOU'RE BEING HYPNOTIZED</u>. That's why huge flat screen TV's and cell phones are dirt cheap. They're readily and easily accessible for all Americans. Those items are made to be very affordable. Did you notice that yet? They're making sure that people get all of their fancy gizmos and toys and there's a reason for that. And there's a reason why your food and rent is so expensive; to keep you busy struggling, that way you won't have time to worry about what the government is doing. "No time for research, I have to go to work!" About half (or more) of the average American worker's income goes for rent costs. The rest is for food, and if they're lucky they might have enough cash in their pocket to go to their fake doctor and get some poison medicine. Public transportation sucks more and more lately too, because they're forcing everyone into their own cars. They aim to both sell more gas and oil, as well as poison

---

[73] https://medicinal-foods.com/decalcify-pineal-gland/

to atmosphere. It helps them control their empire while they crush the population with their poisons, bombarding them on all fronts and cashing in on it all. Gas, oil, fossil fuels, chemical cleansers and detergents, fluoride, so-called medicine such as chemotherapy, liquor, cigarettes – the list goes on concerning their profit-making poisons. Both results work out great for their agenda. More money, more power and a smaller population.

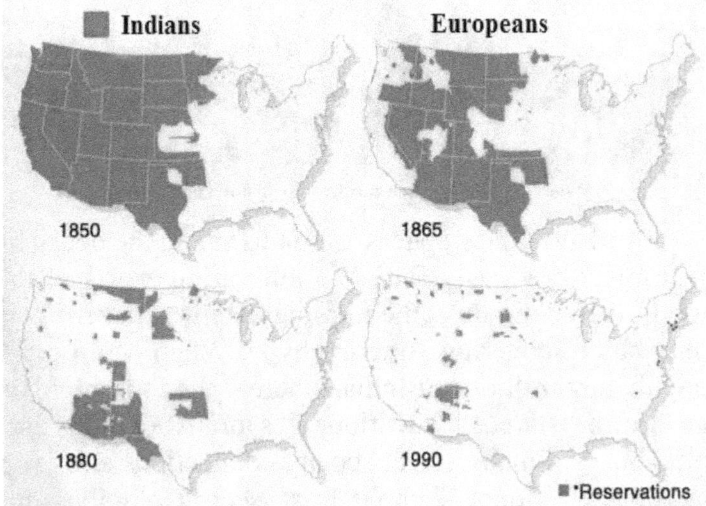

Don't ever say anything that's true about America, or you'll be hated. Of course, those who are hating you are telling you that it's a free country while in reality you can only be free in this country with their permission. The first time you say anything they don't like your imaginary freedom suddenly goes away. All of a sudden you're told "Love it or leave it! Get the fuck out!" If it's a free country why am I being bashed and abused for having my own views? Why am I told to leave the land that I was born in for taking on a different viewpoint that yours? Imagine taking nearly one third of the population of the USA, over 100,000,000 [74] people, and exterminating them. That's how this country was born. First, they slaughtered those (Indian peoples) who were here and then, they paved it over and turned it into a shopping mall.

---

[74] http://www.worldfuturefund.org/Reports/Genocide/genocide.html

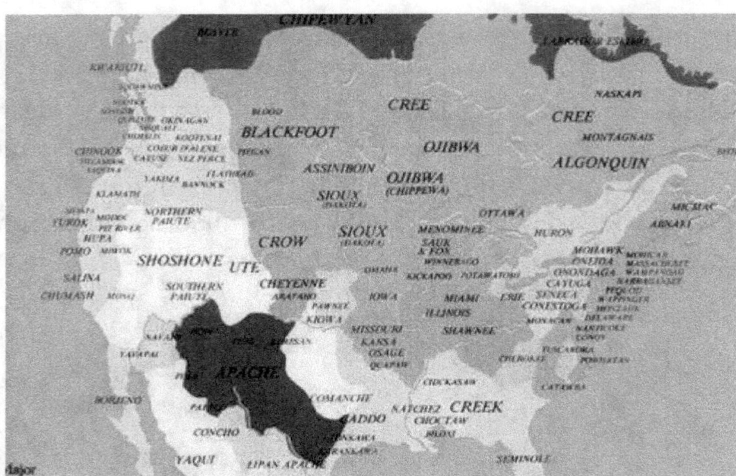

When did you <u>ever</u> see this in your history books in school?

In 1492 Christopher Columbus sailed the ocean blue, but the government obviously forgot to tell various parts of the story. I'll happily fill you in on some missing details. I never bought into the Columbus discovering America hype. When I told my Dad "there were already millions of Indians here!" the look on his face turned sour and he stared at the floor. It's pretty obvious isn't it, Dad? Columbus had many secret society connections and even his father was of the Order of the Christ sect. Columbus himself was connected to an offshoot of the Knights Templar called the Cathars and he flew a flag with a red cross on a white background, the Knights Templar flag, which was outlawed by the Pope at the time due to his removal of them from the church. Columbus was funded by Catholic King Ferdinand and Queen Isabella of Spain and also the de Medici family, high ranking Illuminati[75] members whose family lineage goes all the way back to the King's list of ancient Sumer. The Knights of Christ, which was the Knights Templar by another name in order to hide their identity from the Pope, was in Portugal at the time had a Grand Master called Prince Henry the Navigator. Columbus' father-in-law was the sea captain on one of his ships and had access to many secret maps and other hidden knowledge.[76] Many maps of ancient times indicate that the world was charted thousands of years ago, but was a well-kept secret.

---

[75] Not to be confused with the later sect known as the *Bavarian Illuminati* started by Adam Weishaupt.

[76] *...And the Truth Shall Set You Free* by David Icke

The ancient map of Piri Reis, a Turkish navy Admiral, is one example. It's a map that shows North and South America, Greenland and Antarctica. Drawn up in 1513, only about 20 years after Columbus' voyage, it shows in great detail what the land mass looks like underneath Antarctica. Modern reports state that it was accurate to an amazing degree, indicating prior knowledge from before the ice covered it thousands of years ago. Reis had said that he compiled his map from ones he'd seen made by others from long before, so this makes all the sense in the world, and the US Air Force agrees:

> "...the coastline had been mapped before it was covered by the ice cap."[77]

As documented in the book *Prince Henry Sinclair's Voyage to the New World 1398* by Frederick J. Pohl, numerous whites had already set sail for the Americas. Aside from Prince Henry Sinclair; the Phoenicians, Norse, Irish, Welsh, Bretons, Basques, and Portugese had already arrived there. They had already known of America and their later so-called discovery of North America in 1497 by John Cabot. High ranking Freemason and author Manly P. Hall explains:

> "The explorers who opened the New World operated from a master plan and were agents of re-discovery rather than discoverers. Very little is known about the origin, lives, characters and policies of these intrepid adventurers. Although they lived in a century amply provided with historians and biographers, these saw fit either to remain silent or to invent plausible accounts without substance."[78]

It was all staged, planned and intended to bring about the colonization to the Americas that they desired to make happen, and as I mentioned above, getting the ball rolling by exterminating nearly 100,000,000 Indians over the course of three or four centuries was just the beginning for the Americas as far as these secret brotherhoods were concerned. The USA has been at war with other countries for 224 out of its 241-year existence, making it the most blood thirsty nation in the history of the planet. Right now they have their military spread out all over the world, bombing everyone in sight and setting up over 900 bases in 153 different countries. The USA likes to talk about the threat of nuclear weapons all the time, yet which country has the most? And which country dropped not

---

[77] Lt. Colonel Harold Z. Onlmeyer, Commander, 8 Reconnaisanse Technical Squadron (SAC), US Airforce

[78] *America's Assignment with Destiny, The Adepts in Western Tradition* by Manly P. Hall

one but two bombs on Japan making them the only country ever to nuke another country? Hypocrisy anyone? How many Americans want to volunteer to go live in a country where they have regular air strikes and bombings? Let's send you there for a family vacation, how's that? Why not? You demand that it happens, you demand that I support it, but you won't go live in the middle of it? If you cannot have it done unto yourself then you shouldn't support it being done to other people. Supporting the mass murder of other people for any reason the government wants to make up. Gee, what a concept. Does it make you feel all warm and fuzzy inside?

"Rumsfeld visited Baghdad in 1983 to arrange for the shipment of chemical and biological weapons to Saddam Hussein from the Reagan-Bush administration and in 2000 he was on the board of the European engineering company, ABB, when it supplied nuclear technology to North Korea." - David Icke[79]

The USA arming the rest of the world with billions in weapons sales to foreign countries every year[80] isn't exactly helping to make it a peaceful world. Many of the weapons that were used by Saddam Hussein in the 1991 Gulf War, including his chemical weapons that were talked about so harshly by the USA's press and government, were in fact supplied to him by the USA. And that's common practice for the USA, going to war against people using their own weapons against them.

"I'm so sick of arming the world, then sending troops over to destroy the fucking arms, you know what I mean? We keep arming these little countries, then we go and blow the shit out of them. We're like the bullies of the world. We're like Jack Palance in the movie *Shane*, throwing the pistol at the sheepherder's feet.

---

[79] *Tales From the Time Loop* by David Icke

[80] https://www.defensenews.com/pentagon/2016/11/08/us-weapons-exports-end-2016-at-33-6-billion/

'Pick it up.'
'I don't wanna pick it up mister, you'll shoot me.'
'Pick up the gun.'
'Mister, I don't want no trouble. I just came downtown here to get some hard rock candy for my kids, some gingham for my wife. I ain't looking for no trouble Mister.' 'Pick up the gun.'
[He picks it up, three gunshots ring out.]
'You all saw him. He had a gun.'" - **Bill Hicks**

You all saw Saddam. He had chemical weapons (that he got from the USA!) but there weren't any weapons of mass destruction, that was a lie. Excuse me but I don't think that any of this has anything to do with precious freedom. America is building empire, corporate profits are top priority, it's an offensive mission and defense has absolutely nothing to do with it. America is the bully of the world, that's a verified fact (see the data for yourself on the next six pages). Why not just be honest about what this place is and put in an appropriate candidate for president? Darth Vader would be a President we can rely on to carry on America's age-old traditions—arming dictators and blowing the shit out of innocent civilians. There's nothing more American than that! We can most definitely rely on Darth Vader to carry on with those traditions. Yes, we can!!

US Military "Interventions" Since 1945[81]

List includes USA invasions, bombings and so-called interventions, only since WWII ended!

1945: China
    Germany
    Austria
    Japan
    Philippines
    South Korea
1946: China
    Germany
    Austria
    Japan
    Philippines
1947: China

---

[81] https://en.wikipedia.org/wiki/Timeline_of_United_States_military_operations

Germany
Austria
Japan
France
Italy
Greece
Philippines
Peru
1948: Germany
Austria
Japan
Vietnam
South Korea
Nicaragua
1949: Germany
Austria
Japan
China
1950: Colombia
Korea
Puerto Rico
1951: Korea
1952: Korea
1953: Korea
Philippines
1954: Vietnam
1955: Vietnam
1956: Vietnam
Egypt
1957: Vietnam
Jordan
1958: Vietnam
Lebanon
Indonesia
Japan
1959: Vietnam
Haiti
Nepal
1960: Vietnam
Congo
Cuba
Iraq
1961: Vietnam
Cuba
Dominican Republic
1962: Thailand
Vietnam
Cuba
Brazil
Dominican Republic
1963: Vietnam
Iraq
El Salvador
1964: Vietnam
Panama
1965: Vietnam
Dominican Republic
Indonesia

Laos
Thailand
Peru
1966: Vietnam
Laos
Central Africa
Bolivia
1967: Vietnam
Cuba
1968: Vietnam
1969: Cambodia
Vietnam
1970: Vietnam
Uruguay
Oman
1971: Vietnam
1972: Vietnam
Nicaragua
Australia
Iraq
1973: Cambodia
1974: Vietnam
Zaire
Portugal
1975: Vietnam
East Timor
Iraq
Morocco
1976: Lebanon
Korea
Indonesia
Philippines
1977: Pakistan
Egypt
Zaire
Indonesia
1978: Zaire
Guatemala
1979: Iran
Central Africa
Afghanistan
Cambodia
Vietnam
Yemen
1980: Iran
El Salvador
Honduras
Iraq
Cambodia
Italy
South Korea
1981: Tanzania
El Salvador
Libya
Indo-China
1982: Lebanon
Guatemala
South Africa

        Afghanistan
        Iraq
1983: Chad
        Honduras
        Egypt
        Grenada
        Lebanon
        Nicaragua
        Zimbabwe
1984: Persian Gulf
        Honduras
        Mozambique
1985: Italy
        Lebanon
        New Zealand
        Chad
        Honduras
1986: Honduras
        Nicaragua
        Libya
1987: Persian Gulf
        Honduras
        Iran
1988: Panama
        Persian Gulf
        Iran
        Iraq
        Honduras
        Colombia
        El Salvador
        Turkey
1989: Columbia
        Bolivia
        Peru
        Philippines
        Honduras
        El Salvador
        Panama
        Cambodia
        Libya
1990: Liberia
        Panama
        Nicaragua
        El Salvador
        Guatemala
        Bulgaria
        Germany
1991: Iraq
        Philippines
1992: Iraq
        Kuwait
        Bosnia
        Herzegovina
        Somalia
        Colombia
        Albania
        Angola
1993: Macedonia

Bosnia
Iraq
Cuba
1994: Macedonia
Bosnia
Iraq
Haiti
Jordan
Colombia
1995: Haiti
Bosnia
Turkey
Iraq
Mexico
Iran
1996: Central African Republic
Iraq
Bosnia
Mongolia
1997: Albania
Rwanda
Iraq
1998: Liberia
Afghanistan
Iraq
Sudan
Turkey
Guatemala
South Korea
1999: East Timor
Serbia
Yugoslavia
Iraq
Guatemala
2000: East Timor
Iraq
Kyrgyzstan
2001: East Timor
Colombia
China
Israel
Iraq
Afghanistan
2002: Iraq
Afghanistan
Angola
Yemen
Philippines
2003: Afghanistan
Iraq
Liberia
2004: Georgia
Djibouti
Kenya
Ethiopia
Yemen
Eritrea
Haiti

Iraq
Afghanistan
2005: Pakistan
Iraq
Afghanistan
2006: Pakistan
Lebanon
Iraq
Afghanistan
2007: Iraq
Afghanistan
Somalia
2008: Iraq
Afghanistan
2009: Iraq
Afghanistan
2010: Yemen
Iraq
Afghanistan
2011: Uganda
Yemen
Iraq
Afghanistan
Libya
Pakistan
Somalia
2012: Uganda
Yemen
Iraq
Afghanistan
Jordan
Turkey
Chad
2013: Uganda
Yemen
Iraq
Afghanistan
Somalia
2014: Syria
Iraq
Afghanistan
Uganda
Yemen
Iraq
2015: Syria
Uganda
Yemen
Iraq
Afghanistan
Cameroon
2016: Cameroon
Syria
Uganda
Yemen
Somalia
Pakistan
Iraq
Syria

Libya
Afghanistan
2017: Cameroon
Uganda
Syria
Afghanistan
Somalia
Iraq
Yemen
Libya
2018: Cameroon
Syria
Uganda
Yemen
Iraq
Afghanistan

He has two choices; pick up a gun or die. Put yourself in his shoes.

"Weapons are the tools of violence;
all decent men detest them,
Therefore, followers of the Tao never use them,
Arms serve evil.
They are the tools of those who oppose wise rule.
Use them only as a last resort.
For peace and quiet are dearest to the decent man's heart,
and to him even a victory is no cause for rejoicing.
He who thinks triumph beautiful

> is one with a will to kill,
> and one with a will to kill
> shall never prevail upon the world.
>
> It is a good sign when man's higher nature
> comes forward.
> A bad sign when his lower nature comes forward.
>
> With the slaughter of multitudes
> we have grief and sorrow.
> Every victory is a funeral;
> when you win a war,
> you celebrate by mourning."

- Tao Te Ching, Ancient Chinese Spiritual Text, Verse 31[82]

Meanwhile in Africa, the poor, innocent people over there are getting all of their resources stolen. US Imperialism has devastated their resources.[83] They don't have much of anything to sell and make money with anymore because of the USA (and to be fair, other industrialized nations that are owned and controlled by the same banking families) looting their resources. Africa's not poor by any means as you've been told by your government and in those television ads that promote false information. The whole continent is covered in oil, they have diamonds, gold, platinum, uranium, iron ore, copper, cotton, coffee, cocoa beans, etc.

All of the major oil companies have factories over there as they watch the African people starve; and as a matter of fact the four horsemen of banking that own and control the Federal Reserve; *Bank of America, Wells Fargo, JP Morgan Chase* and *CitiBank*, also own and control the big four oil companies; *Exxon, Chevron, Shell* and *BP*.[84] At the top of the pyramid in ownership the trail always leads back to the same banking families, I'll name them off very soon.

Secret society member and business associate of these banking families, Bill Gates, sent toxic vaccines paralyzing and injuring thousands of kids[85] but they didn't send any food! They don't need toxic vaccines! They need food! Is anybody home McFly? Gates and his vaccines are all a part of the Illuminati's population

---

[82] *Change Your Thoughts, Change Your Life: Living the Wisdom of the Tao* by Dr. Wayne W. Dyer

[83] http://www.globalresearch.ca/us-imperialism-in-africa/5317219

[84] *ZEITGEIST Moving Forward* documentary by Peter Joseph

[85] http://www.theeventchronicle.com/study/depopulation-africa-paralyzing-vaccine-deaths-47500-50-children-recently-paralyzed-bill-gates-meningitis-vaccine/

control[86] agenda that they're implementing over there to kill off the undesirables with no money to contribute to the system. It's the intentional murdering of an entire continent's population. Can Americans tell me why they're sending poisonous vaccines galore but no food is getting sent over there? I didn't think so.

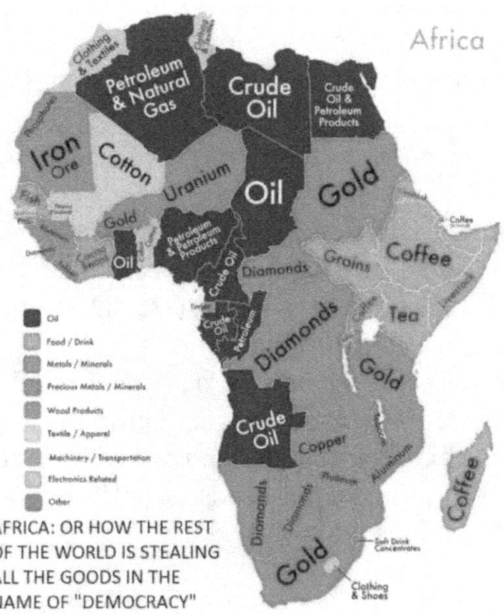

AFRICA: OR HOW THE REST OF THE WORLD IS STEALING ALL THE GOODS IN THE NAME OF "DEMOCRACY"

"The world has 6.8 billion people … that's headed up to about 9 billion. Now if we do a really great job on new vaccines, healthcare, reproductive health services, we could **lower that** by perhaps 10 – 15 percent." - **Bill Gates** (emphasis my own)

Africa is getting looted by this "great free country" and the American people drive tanks everywhere! SUVs, giant pickup trucks, etc., with only one person per vehicle inside. When I pass them on the freeway the SUVs are typically totally empty except for the driver. Americans typically show no remorse or appreciate where their resources are coming from, they're just selfish and most of them have no idea what's going on in Africa anyway. They don't even have a clue. They believe what they're told by our government, that Africa is "just poor." I spent most of my life believing that monumental lie until I learned about these things on the internet quite a few years ago, but I wasn't aware that it was this bad until I was into my 40's because this is such a great free country and we

---

[86] For in depth information on the agenda read Jim Marrs' book *Population Control: How Corporate Owners Are Killing Us*

have such a fine free press giving us such excellent information. I hope that Americans realize that those Africans are starving, by and large, because of you, your pickup trucks, your SUVs and your shameless waste of natural resources! The fact of the matter is that gas, oil and fossil fuels are obsolete technologies and have been since the start, they used those resources to make money and gain power and control, it's not about needing it for anything. Oil was never necessary at all, neither is coal, nuclear or anything else.

> "Electric power is everywhere present in unlimited quantities and can drive the world's machinery without the need of coal, oil, gas, or any other of the common fuels."
> **- Nikola Tesla**

Nikola Tesla was a great man who was written out of history, for the most part. His inventions went against the grain, so they destroyed him. He was an honest scientist and wanted people to know the truth. He died poor.[87]

Additionally, Henry Ford's first Model-T was designed to run on ethyl alcohol extracted from hemp fiber! *Popular Mechanics* documented this fact in 1941 and various videos can be found on *YouTube*.[88] Oil from hemp seeds is sufficient to use in cars as an internal lubricant as well.

> "The fuel of the future (**ethyl alcohol**) is going to come from fruit like that sumach out by the road, or from apples, weeds, sawdust -- almost anything. **There is fuel in every bit of vegetable matter that can be fermented**. There's enough alcohol in one year's yield of an acre of potatoes to drive the machinery necessary to cultivate the fields for a hundred years."
> **- Henry Ford**(emphasis my own)

The technology also exists for cars that run on the following; You can *Google* these: Electricity, H20 car or water powered car, compressed air car. Additionally, any and all current diesel engines can quickly be converted to run on nothing but deep fat fryer oil.[89] Instead of gasoline and oil we could be using all of these combined and never have pollution![90] Ever! The map below shows where America is bombing and looting oil and other resources!

---

[87] https://teslauniverse.com/nikola-tesla/timeline/1943-nikola-tesla-dies-age-86

[88] https://youtu.be/54vD_cPCQM8

[89] www.greasecar.com

[90] See the *ZEITGEIST Moving Forward* documentary on *YouTube* for more information on alternative energy technologies.

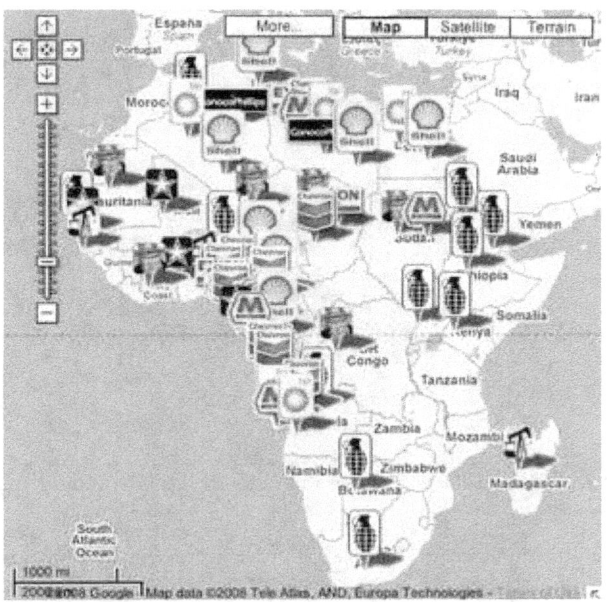

In 1991 during the Gulf War I had a standard **<u>NO WAR</u>** sign hanging up in my apartment window in Olympia, WA. My heart said no to war so I did what everybody else was doing, I expressed my feelings about the war. If they can have flags and yellow ribbons then I can have a **<u>NO WAR</u>** sign. I think that's fair and I think that if this is a free country then there shouldn't be any problems with that. Anyway, one afternoon I heard loud banging on my door... I waited a minute because I was a bit shaken, it was loud! But then I opened up the door and saw someone turn tail and run away like a candy-ass pussy! There was a note taped to the door that said:

"If you don't like the U.S. and our President. Get the fuck out! Go to the Soviet Union! Take sign out of your window! Proud to be an American. A Vietnam Vet."

Thanks so much and you have a nice day too, brother!

"Amerika was built on the slaughter of a people. That is its history... Until we understand the nature of institutional violence and how it manipulates values and mores to maintain the power of a few, we will forever be imprisoned in the caves of ignorance... Become an internationalist and learn to respect all life. Make war on machines, and in particular the sterile machines of the corporate death and the robots that guard them."
- Abbie Hoffman[91]

Support War and Corporatism? Get the fuck off the planet! Go to Mars!

---

[91] *Steal This Book* by Abbie Hoffman

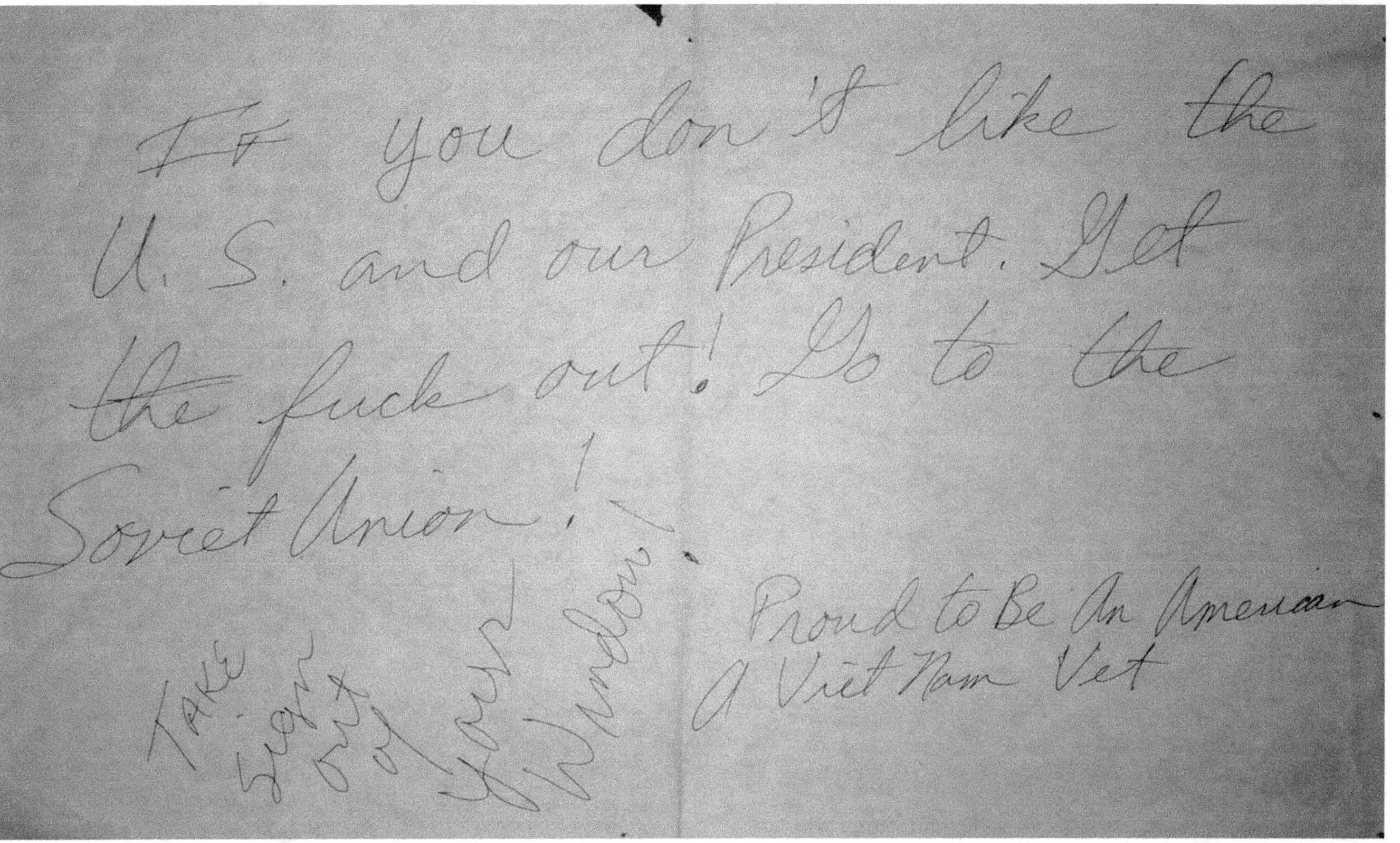
If you don't like the
U.S. and our President. Get
the fuck out! Go to the
Soviet Union!
Take sign out of your Window!
Proud to Be An American
A Viet Nam Vet

Muhammad Ali did the right thing; the man called out his name and he just stood there refusing to acknowledge or step up for induction! He was against the war but he could have kicked anybody's ass in the ring who wanted to call him a coward for it! Who's the pussy now? Having morals and standing up for convictions takes real courage. He was a real man. Even if Muhammad Ali never did anything else in his life, even without the boxing career, he was still a great man for staying true to his heartfelt convictions![92]

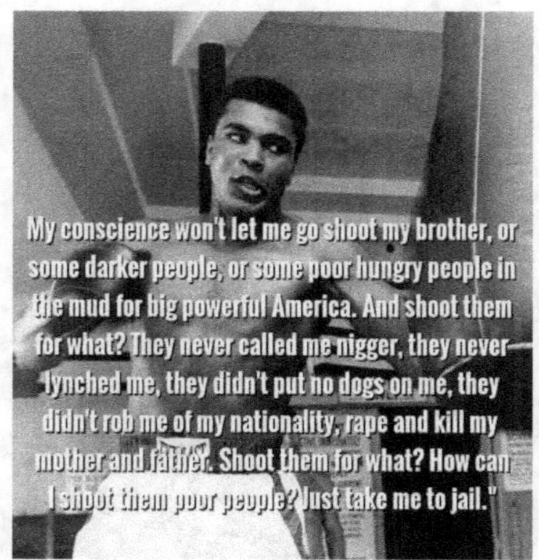

---

[92] R.I.P. Brother. I love you man! Thanks for being a fine example of greatness of character for me to refer to!

Peace is terribly, terribly offensive to the American public.

During the same period, I wore one of those peace-flag buttons on my jacket everywhere I went. Nothing else, just a black leather jacket, long hair, and one of those buttons. You wouldn't believe some of the hard stares and glares that I had to endure on the streets of Olympia, WA. Why were Americans glaring at me on the streets and giving me arrogant, condescending looks? My heart says that blowing up innocent people with bombs is wrong, so they're going to hate my guts for it. I see how that works! Americans are such good people! I went to order up a burger at a fast food joint once and the girl behind the counter gave me a dirty look that would kill. I was young, only twenty-three years old, and I hadn't yet figured out that this is a tyrannical dictatorship with a brainwashed population. I thought that I actually had a right to say how I felt. I thought that my fellow Americans would respect my views and my feelings. I was wrong, they don't. They have a very low tolerance for indisputable facts and evidence too! They'll have a denial festival in your honor on *FaceBook* with you as the butt of all their jokes if you post up anything that's true and correct. They'll gang up on you and then give each other virtual high fives. According to many Americans, being "too political" is a terrible offense. According to these people, if you care about the world enough to get involved, then you're just far too negative of a person, especially if what you post goes against the government's official line, then they'll hate your guts even more. If you have the facts on your side, they'll call you a bully rather than accept the information as true. They'll leave you rude comments and block you. They'd rather be ignorant and avoid any and all involvement and discussion. They turn a blind eye and a deaf ear and then scold people like me for posting factually true and correct information. I'm not supposed to do that, it's "too negative" they say. Anything but face the facts!

When I was a young boy, I loved collecting baseball cards. I was a baseball fan and little league player like every normal American boy. I grew up loving Pete Rose, Johnny Bench, Reggie Jackson, Carl Yastremski; I actually got to meet Cal Ripken Jr. at the ballpark one year. That was awesome! I've always loved baseball! But umm, *what the hell is this*? Training young minds to love war, I see, we have to get them started early! The more brainwashing they get the better! Gotta start in on 'em young! In George Orwell's society (*1984*) war was peace too!

"Coalition for Peace"

"America, fuck yeah! Comin' again to save the motherfuckin' day, yeah!"
- **Team America: World Police**

Will you trade me your Ken Griffey, Jr. Rookie card for a Commander in Chief and a Tomahawk Cruise Missile?

"We have become a Nazi monster in the eyes of the whole world. A nation of bullies and bastards who would rather kill than live peacefully. We are not just whores for power and oil, but killer whores with hate and fear in our hearts. We are human scum, and that is how history will judge us. No redeeming social value, just whores. Get out of our way or we'll kill you." - **Hunter S. Thompson**

"The Bellamy salute is a salute described by Francis Bellamy, the author of the American Pledge of Allegiance, as the gesture which was to accompany the pledge. During the period when it was used with the Pledge of Allegiance, it was sometimes known as the 'flag salute.' Both the Pledge and its salute originated in 1892. Later, during the 1920s and 1930s, Italian fascists and Nazis adopted a salute which was very similar, and which was derived from the Roman salute, a gesture that was popularly (albeit erroneously) believed to have been used in ancient Rome. This resulted in controversy over the use of the Bellamy salute in the United States. It was officially replaced by the hand-over-heart salute when Congress amended the Flag Code on December 22, 1942."[93]

Hitler first adopted his Nazi salute by copying the USA. It wasn't always the hand over the heart you know! The Pledge of Allegiance is a hypnotic mind-control technique. They've been **<u>HYPNOTIZING</u>** you! Think about it:

1) Stand at attention
2) Put hand on heart
3) Stare at flag
4) Recite a hypnotic verse
5) Repeat daily

Not to mention the Star Spangle Banner at every baseball game, football game, etc. and if somebody doesn't "salute the flag properly" typical Americans get offended. They're hypnotized! American Christians are offended by swear words but they're perfectly OK with war, blowing the shit out of innocent women and children is perfectly OK with them. War good. Swearing bad. War good. Not worshiping flag bad. Words are words. Nobody dies when

---

[93] https://en.wikipedia.org/wiki/Bellamy_salute

I say fuck or shit or goddammit, those are words. And nobody dies when I refuse to salute a stupid flag but many people die in America's wars! Don't you think that those backwards priorities indicate brainwashing?

WAR IS PEACE
FREEDOM IS SLAVERY
IGNORANCE IS STRENGTH

Let me run you through this and prove to you that typical Americans are mostly all mind-controlled, brainwashed slaves just like the victims of George Orwell's *1984* society and the people of Nazi Germany.

1) Americans believe that wars create peace (**War is Peace**) I've already shown that in America you're not allowed to be against war. Everybody hates you for that. This is a WAR based society and everybody is brainwashed to believe it is for the purpose of peace in the world! First point proven!

2) They also believe that they're "free" even though they're being systematically poisoned by the government and cancer cures are being covered up simultaneously, meanwhile they put people to death with chemotherapy left and right in plain view of everyone and nobody bats an eye. Instead of putting people in ovens, they're using chemotherapy. (**Freedom is Slavery**)

3) The American people argue with facts and evidence, reject true and correct information, and gang up on people who present the truth! (**Ignorance is Strength**)

I wouldn't be writing this book if it wasn't for the war on information that typical Americans are waging with their brainwashed slant and bias! They clearly do not want to be educated or in the know! They argue and fight against it!

And don't ever say anything that's verified correct about the medical establishment, the drugs that the FDA approves for new born babies, the dogmatic, slanted science that they present for vaccines, the schools getting paid to hand out Ritalin to kids[94] or anything like that or you'll be absolutely despised as well. If you try to protect America's children typical American parents will hate your guts. Never, ever try to protect their children, that's a major offense.

"I have a very fine doctor in charge of my children's care, they'll be OK. The other four were vaccinated and they're OK too..."

---

[94] http://www.rense.com/general4/addd.htm

...as they glare at you like you're the spawn of Satan, being arrogantly defensive, refusing to hear anything that's being said, hating your guts for pointing out true and correct science. The claim that "my kids are OK therefore vaccines must be OK" doesn't hold up under the rules of logic. It's not logical because with their defensive bias they've removed evidence from the table. They've ignored kids who were injured and only pointed towards their own uninjured kids. Not logical. These people are very brainwashed, arguing in favor of poisoning their own children! Very irrational too! That's an absolute sign of **HYPNOSIS**! I'll show them the list of ingredients and they'll just argue with me! Or snicker! They won't look at it! They have absolutely no interest in knowing what their innocent children are about to receive in their shots! They don't care about their own children apparently! They're thinking "Oh, the doctor knows...." as they blatantly avoid and ignore the ingredients. They'd much rather trust authority figures and call me a conspiracy theorist than pay attention and protect their own children! Here's the list straight from CDC.gov:

"Common substances found in vaccines include:

- **Aluminum**: gels or salts of aluminum which are added as adjuvants to help the vaccine stimulate a better response. Adjuvants help promote an earlier, more potent response, and more persistent immune response to the vaccine.

- **Antibiotics**: which are added to some vaccines to prevent the growth of germs (bacteria) during production and storage of the vaccine. No vaccine produced in the United States contains penicillin.

- **Egg protein**: is found in influenza and yellow fever vaccines, which are prepared using chicken eggs. Ordinarily, persons who are able to eat eggs or egg products safely can receive these vaccines.

- **Formaldehyde**: is used to inactivate bacterial products for toxoid vaccines, (these are vaccines that use an inactive bacterial toxin to produce immunity.) It is also used to kill unwanted viruses and bacteria that might contaminate the vaccine during production.

- **Monosodium glutamate (MSG) and 2-phenoxy-ethanol**: which are used as stabilizers in a few vaccines to help the vaccine remain unchanged when the vaccine is exposed to heat, light, acidity, or humidity.

- **Thimerosal**: is a mercury-containing preservative that is added to vials of vaccine that contain more than one dose to prevent contamination and growth of potentially harmful bacteria.

For children with a prior history of allergic reactions to any of these substances in vaccines, parents should consult their child's healthcare provider before vaccination."

Yep and have a good time taking care of your child when they come down with autism or leukemia, you won't have much time for football then! Your day will be full of appointments, appointments, appointments with sick kids in the car and more so-called medicines to pick up at the pharmacy all because you wouldn't pay attention to what's in your child's shots! Before you approve these poisonous shots for your kids, keep in mind that there is no safe dosage level for formaldehyde, it can cause leukemia and other cancers, as well as nervous system damage, brain damage, blindness and seizures. MSG is a brain toxin that attacks neurons, and putting aluminum in the blood stream is one of the worst things that you can do to a human being. Aluminum poisoning causes the loss of intellectual function; forgetfulness, memory loss, inability to concentrate, and in extreme cases, full blown dementia. And isn't it interesting that many of the symptoms related to most of the above vaccine ingredients correlate with and are almost identical to the symptoms of autism?

> "Did you know that the FDA Safety Level for Aluminum Exposure on a brand new child is 20 micrograms? That's the FDA safety level, meaning anything over 20 micrograms can cause severe neurological injury for an infant. Did you know that the shot given in the hospital before a baby is released, the Hepatitis B vaccine, contains 225 micrograms of aluminum? I bet you didn't know that. And you know what the problem is? Most parents don't know that." - **Mary Tocco**[95]

They usually give that shot to babies on the first day of life! Never mind that it contains 11 times the limit set by the FDA for safety, and never mind that the child's blood-brain barrier isn't working yet! Now go back and look at the symptoms of aluminum poisoning again. Go ahead, I'll wait... As if aluminum isn't enough to worry about, we also have mercury, one of the most toxic and poisonous substances known to humankind as an ingredient in a shot that they give to infants! Did you know that there are 25 mcg of mercury included in almost every vaccine while the EPA sets the toxicity limit of mercury at .1 mcg? I'll do the math for you; almost every vaccine contains 250 times the toxicity limit of mercury set by the EPA. As far as the so-called mercury free ones are concerned the FDA made a new rule stating that the vaccine manufacturers don't have to list it as an ingredient on the label unless it's used as a preservative! Most vaccines do, in fact, still contain, at the bare minimum trace amounts of mercury. The symptoms of mercury poisoning include:

---

[95] Vaccine expert for over 30 years, owner and operator of ChildhoodShots.com

- Loss of speech
- Social withdrawl
- Reduced eye contact
- Repetitive behaviors
- Hand-flapping, Toe walking
- Temper tantrums
- Sleep disturbances
- Seizures

The symptoms of autism include:

- Loss of speech
- Social withdrawl
- Reduced eye contact
- Repetitive behaviors
- Hand-flapping, Toe walking
- Temper tantrums
- Sleep disturbances
- Seizures

I'd also like to throw in a tidbit concerning amalgam mercury fillings.

"Inhaled vapor from amalgam dental fillings crosses the blood-brain barrier, reaching the central nervous system, affecting behavior and personality."
- International Academy of Oral Medicine and Toxicology

Most toothaches can be taken care of with high dosage Echinacea Root and Goldenseal Root combined, which kills off the infection and takes down the swelling, followed by smaller doses every day for a good week or two. Those two herbs combined are perhaps the greatest natural antibiotics on the planet!

Despite the claims of removing mercury from vaccines in the early 2000's, cases of autism have only been skyrocketing. In 1983, according to the CDC's official vaccine schedule, there were a total of only 10 vaccines given to children under the age of 6 and the autism rate was only **1 in 10,000**. As of 2008 there were 36 vaccines given to children under the age of 6 and the autism rate had gone up to **1 in 150**. In 2014 there were 49 vaccines given to children under the age of 6 and we saw **1 in 68**. In the year 2017 53 vaccines were given to children under age six and saw the autism rate go up to **1 in 36**![96] The USA is not only # 1 in killing children, it's # 1 in giving them autism with bullshit vaccines. Autism is an epidemic in this country. It seems everyone knows someone who has an autistic child these days. We can't just ignore the ingredients in vaccines and the

---

[96] www.cdc.gov/vaccines/vac-gen/additives.htm

correlations between higher numbers of vaccines and higher rates of autism. Allow me to point out the fact that most of the ingredients that I mentioned above are toxic to brain function. Go back and read it one more time! And even if mercury really was removed from the vaccines, the other ingredients still remain! Look at this massive list of toxic shit! And keep in mind that typical American parents will just gloss right over it when shown, act like it's no big deal, and then take their kids straight to the pediatrician to get vaccinated anyway! Common sense is optional to be a parent these days! So is research! I feel sorry for America's children! I really do! How about getting a clue, American parents? How about getting your shit together? Additional ingredients unfit for human consumption include:

2-Phenoxyethanol: A carcinogen, a developmental and reproductive toxicant, a metabolic poison that interferes with the metabolism of all cells, the primary factor in the formation of cancer cells. It disables the immune system.

Ammonium Sulfate: A carcinogen. Prepared by mixing ammonia with sulfuric acid. Used as a chemical fertilizer for alkaline soils to lower thepH. In the body it stresses the immune system by causing acidosis. Is a liver toxicant, neurotoxicant, and respiratory toxicant.

Amphotericin B: Can cause irreversible kidney damage and liver failure. It has been known to produce severe histamine (allergic) reactions. There are several reports of anemia and cardiac failure. Other side effects include blood clots, blood defects, kidney problems, nausea and fever. When used on the skin, allergic reactions can occur.

Animal Organ Tissue and Animal Blood: Animal cells are used to culture the viruses in vaccines and contain many types of animal viruses including monkey (kidney), cow (heart), calf (serum), chicken (embryo and egg), duck (egg), pig (blood), sheep (blood), dog (kidney), horse (blood), rabbit (brain), and guinea pig.

Animal Viruses: The most documented is the monkey virus SV40. The virus is harmless in monkeys but it stimulates rare cancers when injected into humans; brain cancer, bone (multiple myeloma), lungs (mesothelioma), and lymphoid tissue (lymphoma).

Antifreeze (ethylene glycol): Like what you put in your car! A carcinogen; it is a cardiovascular or blood toxicant, endocrine toxicant, gastrointestinal toxicant, liver toxicant and neurological toxicant. Classified as a "very toxic material."

Aspartame (Artificial Sweetener): A carcinogen. Converts to formaldehyde in the body. Many side effects include headache, dizziness, nausea, abdominal pain, blurred vision, memory loss, fatigue, hives, itching, numbness, breathing difficulty and seizures.

Beta-Propiolactone: A carcinogen, gastrointestinal and liver toxicant, respiratory toxicant, skin toxicant, and sense organ toxicant. More hazardous   than most chemicals earning a 3 out of 3 in ranking systems and appears on at least 5 federal regulatory lists. It is ranked as one of the most hazardous compounds to humans.

Borax (sodium tetraborate decahydrate): A carcinogen traditionally used as a pesticide, it is a cardiovascular or blood toxicant, endocrine toxicant, gastrointestinal toxicant, liver toxicant and neurological toxicant. It was found to cause reproductive damage and reduced fertility in rats. It is banned in foods in the United States due to its toxicity. It is toxic to all cells, and has a slow excretion rate through the kidneys.

Foreign DNA: DNA from animals, viruses, fungi, and bacteria. Again, this is hazardous to the human body and alters DNA!

Genetically Modified Yeast: Genetically modified *anything* is hazardous to the human body and alters DNA!

Glutaraldehyde: A carcinogen. Toxic, causing severe eye, nose, throat and lung irritations, along with headaches, drowsiness, and dizziness. The effects mirror the chemical warfare agent known as nerve gas. It is poisonous if ingested, and known to cause birth defects in experimental animals.

Large Foreign Proteins: In addition to the animal tissue impurities there are large proteins that are deliberately included and used as adjuvants. Egg albumin and gelatin are in several vaccines. Casein (a milk protein) is in the triple antigen (DPT) vaccine. When injected these normally harmless proteins are toxic to the body.

Latex: Latex in vaccines triggers allergic reactions to common products like baby pacifiers and is associated with the rise in those kind of allergies.

Live Human Viruses: Live viruses in vaccines are sometimes claimed to be killed, inactivated, or attenuated. Not true. The method used to inactivate viruses is treatment with formaldehyde. Once injected into the body the formaldehyde is broken down releasing the virus in its original state. It is documented in orthodox medical literature that the "crippled" viruses can revert to their former virulence, which explains why vaccines cause the very diseases they supposedly prevent.

Methanol: A volatile, flammable, poisonous liquid alcohol. It is used as a solvent in industry and as an antifreeze compound in fuel. In the body it is metabolized into formaldehyde.

Mycoplasma: Microscopic organisms are considered to be the smallest free-moving organisms. Many are pathogenic, and one species is the cause of mycoplasma pneumonia which is noted to occur "only in children and young adults" according to *Mosby's Medical Dictionary*.

Phenol: A carcinogen and a cardiovascular and blood toxicant, a developmental toxin, gastrointestinal toxin, liver toxin, kidney toxin, neurotoxin, respiratory toxin, skin and sense organ toxin. It has been placed on at least 8 federal regulatory watch lists.

Polysorbate 20/80 Emulsifier: A known skin and sense organ toxin. Verified as a cancer-causing agent in animals; carcinogen.

Sorbitol (Artifical Sweetener): A carcinogen. Diabetic retinopathy and neuropathy may be related to excess sorbitol in the cells of the eyes and nerves leading to blindness. Sorbitol is a gastrointestinal and liver toxicant.

Sulfate and Phosphate Compounds: Can trigger severe allergies in children which may last throughout their lives to permanently impair their immune systems.

Tri(n)butylphosphate: A carcinogen, a kidney toxicant and a neurotoxicant. It is more hazardous than most chemicals in 2 out of 3 ranking systems. It is on at least 1 federal regulatory list.[97]

---

[97] www.cdc.gov/vaccines/vac-gen/additives.htm

Welcome to the USA, Earth kid. Congratulations on being born in the land of freedom. Mandatory death shots loaded up with carcinogenic chemicals are here. These people are morons. Enjoy your stay.[98]

Here's a brilliant idea; let's put **<u>Borax into a syringe</u>** and inject it into newborn babies! And while we're at it, let's put monkey viruses in it too! And remember – as soon as your child gets leukemia the first thing they'll say is:

"We have to start chemotherapy as soon as possible, there's no time to waste!"

…as they bully and harass parents into accepting chemo. They demand that those children receive so-called "proper care" and they accuse parents who refuse chemo for their children of being unfit parents! But if you have any intelligence whatsoever all that you have to say is:

"Let me see your scientific studies, doc, proving that nitrogen mustard gas cures cancer and promotes physical health and well-being in human biology. As soon as you've provided that scientific proof you can administer it to my child, **but not before then**. I'll see you in court if necessary because I have scientific literature of my own that proves chemotherapy to be a fraud and a death sentence by prescription."

The CDC publicly acknowledged on their website that the vaccines are tainted with cancer causing Simian Virus 40 from monkey kidney tissue (SV40) but then pulled it back down suddenly. It does still exist on the web in archive form.[99]

<u>**Cancer, Simian Virus 40 (SV40), and Polio Vaccine Fact Sheet**</u>

- SV40 is a virus found in some species of monkey.

- SV40 was discovered in 1960. Soon afterward, the virus was found in polio vaccine.and 98 million Americans received one or more doses of polio vaccine from 1955 to 1963 when a proportion of vaccine was contaminated with SV40; it has been estimated that 10–30 million Americans could have received an

---

[98] This is why I feel very blessed NOT to have any kids.

[99] http://web.archive.org/web/20130522091608/http://www.cdc.gov/vaccinesafety/updates/archive/polio_and_cancer_factsheet.htm

SV40 contaminated dose of vaccine. s has been found in certain types of cancer in humans, but it has not been determined that SV40 causes these cancers. fic evidence suggests that SV40-contaminated vaccine did not cause cancer; however, some research results are conflicting[100] and more studies are needed. cines being used today do not contain SV40. All of the current evidence indicates that polio vaccines have been free of SV40 since 1963.

- In the 1950s, rhesus monkey kidney cells, which contain SV40 if the animal is infected, were used in preparing polio vaccines. Because SV40 was not discovered until 1960, no one was aware in the 1950s that polio vaccine could be contaminated.

- SV40 was found in the injected form of the polio vaccine (IPV), not the kind given by mouth (OPV).

- Not all doses of IPV were contaminated. It has been estimated that 10–30 million people actually received a vaccine that contained SV40.

- Some evidence suggests that receipt of SV40-contaminated polio vaccine may increase risk of cancer. However, the majority of studies done in the U.S. and Europe which compare persons who received SV40-contaminated polio vaccine with those who did not have shown no causal relationship between receipt of SV40-contaminated polio vaccine and cancer."

As you can see above, when they posted this up they tried to deny that the vaccines were causing cancers, yet at the same time admitting that they were contaminated with SV40. I don't know exactly how long they had this up on their page, but as I mentioned, they did eventually pull it down. Cancer enzymes have been found in vaccines since the 1950s [101] and when routine vaccination first started cases of leukemia went through the roof. Before vaccination childhood leukemia was rarely even heard of.

"Within a few years of the polio vaccine we started seeing some strange phenomena like the year before the first 300,000 doses were given in the United States childhood leukemia had never struck in children under the age of two. One year after the first onslaught they had the first cases of children under age of two that died of leukemia. Dr. Herbert Radnor observed that in a small area of this little town, in an area where no cases of leukemia had been expected or at the most one in four years according to previous statistics, they suddenly had a rash like an epidemic within a few blocks." - **Eva Snead, M.D.**

"Cancer was practically unknown until compulsory vaccination with cowpox began to be introduced. I have had to deal with at least 200 cases of cancer, and never saw a case of cancer in an unvaccinated person." - **Eustace Mullins**

"The chief, if not the sole cause of the monstrous increase in cancer has been vaccination." - **Dr. Robert Bell**

---

[100] "Some research results are **conflicting**" is another way of saying "but some research results **do indicate** that SV40 causes cancer." So there you have it, even the CDC admit that SV40 **causes cancer according to some studies.**

[101] https://www.ncbi.nlm.nih.gov/pubmed/10472327

"Vaccination and sulfa drugs have been recognized as being directly responsible for production of leukemia in humans." - **Dr. B. Dupperat**

"Many here voice a silent view that the Salk and Sabin vaccine, being made of monkey kidney tissue...has been directly responsible for the major increase in leukemia in this country." - **Dr. F. Klenner**

And as I briefly mentioned earlier in the text, naturopathic doctors discovered nagalase in vaccines:

"...research involving nagalase, **an enzyme/protein made by cancer cells** and viruses that cause immunodeficiency syndromes and autism."[102]

ALERT!! ALERT!! ALERT!! ALERT!!

NAZI SCIENTISTS WERE IMPORTED TO THE USA IMMEDIATELY AFTER WWII, **THEY INVENTED YOUR VACCINES!**

Just some good old boys straight from Nazi Germany getting ready to mass produce and distribute your vaccines among other things like weapons.

OPERATION PAPERCLIP:[103]

A secret CIA program in which more than 1600 NAZI scientists, engineers, and technicians were recruited for US government employment at the end of WWII. Nazi Party members were moved from Germany to the USA for immediate employment.[104]

Prior to 1945 there had only been eleven vaccines produced, six of which were produced during the 20th century. The 1800s brought us vaccines for cholera, rabies, tetanus, typhoid fever and bubonic plague. The 1900s prior to WWII ending brought us vaccines for tuberculosis, diphtheria, pertussis, yellow fever, typhus and tick-borne encephalitus. And so as you can see, we didn't even have a flu vaccine until 1945, which is the very same year that Operation Paperclip got underway. It wasn't until afterwards that we saw massive vaccines being produced and distributed nation-wide on a routine basis.

---

[102] http://www.naturalnews.com/055347_vaccines_dead_doctors_cancer_enzymes.html

[103] *Operation Paperclip: The Secret Intelligence Program That Brought Nazi Scientists to America* by Annie Jacobsen

[104] Go to CIA.gov and type in "Operation Paperclip"

Giving your kids mercury, aluminum, formaldehyde and a long list of other autism and leukemia causing carcinogens and poisons in a shot, and then getting angry with someone pointing out to you what you're doing to your kids isn't very intelligent conduct and are certainly not very good parenting skills. Nazis created them but don't worry, the CDC says they're safe!

"The CDC is not an independent agency. **It is a vaccine company**. The CDC own over 20 vaccine patents. It sells about 4.6 billion dollars of vaccines per year.' .- **Robert F. Kennedy, Jr.** (emphasis my own)

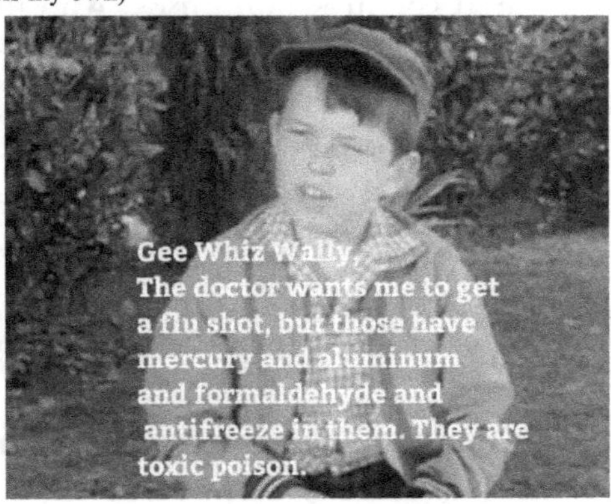

Here's a novel idea; instead of trusting the CDC and their fake vaccine schedule designed to sell more vaccines, try protecting your children. Try being responsible parents, I'm tired of seeing your children's lives being destroyed and everyone ignoring the real reasons why. These innocent children are far more important than being right about your precious vaccine theory. You're wrong, face the facts and stop allowing your children to be murdered. People won't concede the facts even when it comes to the safety of their own children and then they watch their children suffer at the hands of the medical system. They're arrogantly sure of themselves when their kids are healthy but when their kids become autistic, they've got nothing to say, they get quiet all of a sudden. Oops! Well, guess what. You can't take it back now, it's too late. Based upon the long list of neurotoxins and brain damage inducing substances that they contain I really don't think it's much of a stretch to say that vaccines are causing the rise in autism. I really don't believe that fact should be considered controversial! I do believe it's as obvious as the sky being blue that vaccines cause autism. As a matter of fact, on the package insert of the *Sanoi Pasteur DTaP vaccine (Diphtheria,*

Tetanus and Pertussis) dated from Dec. 2005 says the following:

> "Adverse events reported during post-approval use of Tripedia vaccine include idiopathic thrombocytopenic, purpura, **SIDS (sudden infant death syndrome)**, anaphylactic reaction (a severe, life threatening allergic reaction), cellulitis, **autism**, **convulsion/grand mal convulsion**, encephalopathy, hypotonia, neuropathy, somnolence and apnea. Events were included in this list because of the **seriousness or frequency of reporting**." (emphasis my own)

That is an actual package insert on a vaccine openly admitting that it causes SIDS, autism, life threatening allergic reactions, grand mal seizures and more! And then it says that they put those warnings on there because of the frequency and seriousness of the reports that they've received! The list of ingredients on the insert says:

> "Diphtheria and Tetanus Toxoids and Acellular Pertussis Vaccine Absorbed
> Tripedia, Sanofi Pasteur, Inc., Dec. 2005: sodium phosphate, peptone-based medium, bovine extract (US sourced), formaldehyde, ammonium sulfate, aluminum potassium sulfate, modified Mueller and Miller medium, modified Stainer-Scholte medium, isotonic sodium, chloride solution, sodium phosphate, **thimerosal** (trace*)*, gelatin, polysorbate 80 (Tween 80), formaldehyde, aluminum" (emphasis my own)

Take note that they also admit to trace amounts of mercury despite the claim that mercury was removed from vaccines in the early 2000's and even the FDA admits that mercury is still used in vaccines on its website:

> "While the use of mercury-containing preservatives has declined in recent years with the development of new products formulated with alternative or no preservatives, **thimerosal** has been used in some immune globulin preparations, anti-venins, skin test antigens, and ophthalmic and nasal products, in addition to certain **vaccines**." (emphasis my own)[105]

A recent study from April of 2012 clearly demonstrated that *Baby Monkeys Develop Autism Symptoms After Getting Popular Childhood Vaccines*:

> "Following a recent study conducted by scientists at the University of Pittsburgh, Pennsylvania which revealed that many infant monkeys given standard doses of childhood vaccines as part of the new research, developed autism symptoms, question marks over the ultimate safety of vaccines have come to the fore. The groundbreaking research findings presented at the International Meeting for Autism Research (IMFAR) in London, England, have revealed that young macaque monkeys given the typical CDC-recommended vaccination schedule from the 1990s, and in appropriate doses for the monkeys' sizes and ages, tended to develop autism symptoms. Their unvaccinated counterparts, on the other hand, developed no such symptoms, which points to a strong connection between vaccines and autism spectrum disorders."[106]

---

[105] http://www.fda.gov/BiologicsBloodVaccines/SafetyAvailability/VaccineSafety/UCM096228#thi

[106] http://www.fhfn.org/baby-monkeys-develop-autism-symptoms-after-getting-popular-childhood-vaccines/

The great actor Robert DeNiro's son "changed overnight" from a thimerosal containing vaccine. He teamed up with Robert F. Kennedy, Jr. and offered **$100,000.00** to anyone who can prove that vaccines are safe:

> "On one hand, the government is telling pregnant women which mercury-laced fish to avoid so that they don't harm their fetuses, and on the other, the CDC supports injecting mercury-containing vaccines into pregnant women, infants and children," Kennedy said. "This defies all logic and common sense."

There haven't been any winners and there won't be.[107] Also take note of the film *VAXXED* that is available online at this link.[108] The film is considered controversial because it exposes the truth for all to see. The truth is such a terrible thing, especially if it highlights how we're killing our own children, right?

> "We would much rather allow our children to be poisoned to death and suffer than learn the truth about vaccines." - **Typical American Parents**

When I was young, they didn't give many vaccines. Now they give a ton. They're adding vaccines onto that schedule left and right. Vaccine ingredients are included here, and the facts debunk their theory. Vaccines don't prevent illness, they cause it. They cause lots of other fun things too, like autism, leukemia and death. Never cave in to those bullshit laws. If you have any intelligence, you'll fight tooth and nail against the mandatory poisoning of your child, you'll go all the way to the Supreme Court if you have to. There are still religious and philosophical exemptions in most states:

> "All 50 states have legislation requiring specified vaccines for students. Although exemptions vary from state to state, all school immunization laws grant exemptions to children for medical reasons. Almost all states grant religious exemptions for people who have religious beliefs against immunizations.Currently, 18 states allow philosophical exemptions for those who object to immunizations because of personal, moral or other beliefs."[109]

It's mandatory to poison your kids in 3 states now!! Many typical American parents use the tyrannical laws as a quick and convenient excuse to comply. It's more convenient to allow their children to be poisoned.

---

[107] http://www.nydailynews.com/entertainment/de-niro-kennedy-offer-100g-proof-vaccines-safe-article-1.2973956

[108] http://vaxxedthemovie.com/

[109] http://www.ncsl.org/research/health/school-immunization-exemption-state-laws.aspx

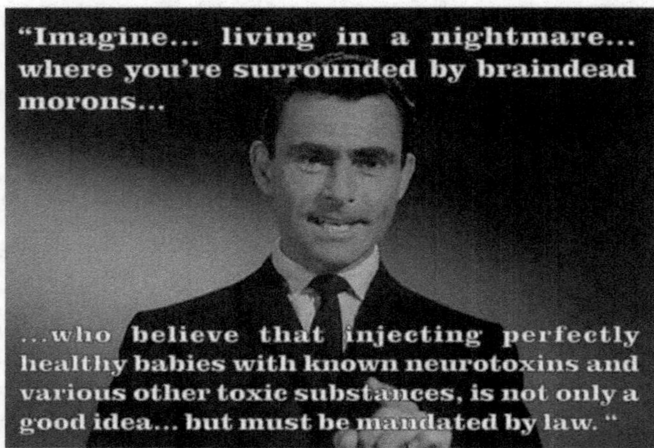

"Vaccination is a barbarous practice and one of the most fatal of all the delusions current in our time. Conscientious objectors to vaccinations should stand alone, if need be, against the whole word, in defense of their conviction." - **Mahatma Gandhi**

Kids that are vaccinated get sick far more than those who aren't vaccinated.[110]

"...the kids that come to me from other practices and are fully vaccinated, often are the kids with asthma, panic disorders, OCD, PANDAS, autism and Aspergers. My kids who never have been vaccinated in my practice, I don't see those issues. I don't have one child who was not vaccinated who also has asthma or food allergies or Asperger's or autism or Crohn's or ulcerative colitis." - **Dr. Toni Bark, M.D.**

---

[110] http://www.vaccinesrevealed.com/news/studies-prove-without-doubt-that-unvaccinated-children-are-healthier-than-their-vaccinated-peers/

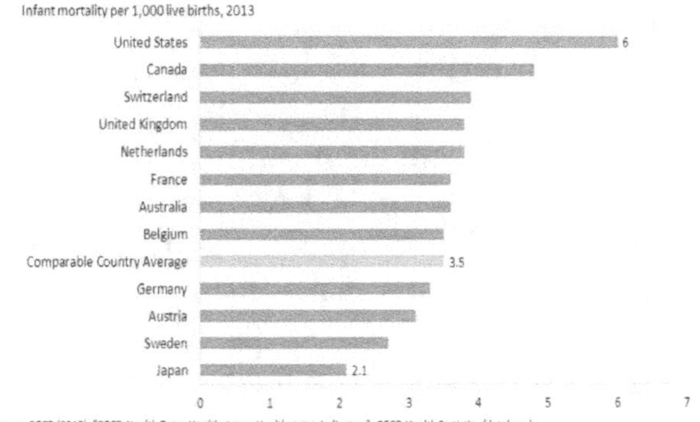

Source: OECD (2013), "OECD Health Data: Health status: Health status indicators", OECD Health Statistics (database). doi: 10.1787/data-00349-en (Accessed on August 6, 2015). And National Vital Statistics System, National Center for Health Statistics, Centers for Disease Control and Prevention Notes: Comparable countries are defined as those with above median GDP and above median GDP per capita in at least one of the past 10 years. In cases where 2013 data were unavailable, data from the last available year are shown. 2013 data for the U.S. are from the National Vital Statistics System.

Graveyard plots are full of children who didn't make it past their first year of life because of vaccines.[111] The USA is also # 1 in killing newborns on their first day of life in the industrialized world because they give the most vaccines.[112]

Take note that Japan is the country that gives the least vaccines and has the lowest death rates, while the USA gives the most vaccines and has the highest death rates. How about that? Pretty interesting isn't it? It should be, if you're a decent parent as opposed to a typical American football zombie. Again, if you're not sticking up for your child, you're a lousy parent. And I mean that, it comes from the very bottom of my heart. Making no effort to save your child is negligence and child abuse. Ignoring warnings about vaccines is the same.

The next step after poisoning the child with vaccines and giving them leukemia is finishing the job with chemotherapy. That's how the state kills innocent children and many adults too, Hitler used ovens, the Illuminati use drugs, toxins, poisons, wars, biological warfare, and what do you think chemotherapy is, chopped liver? Common sense is optional when it comes to cancer treatments

---

[111] https://www.washingtonpost.com/news/wonk/wp/2014/09/29/our-infant-mortality-rate-is-a-national-embarrassment/?utm_term=.05dfbbf6ed2b

[112] https://www.cbsnews.com/news/us-has-highest-first-day-infant-mortality-out-of-industrialized-world-group-reports/

because it serves their interests both financially and in terms of population control to first take their money for the treatments and then put them six feet under to reduce the population. It works out really well for them and their diabolical plan. Those children's hospitals aren't hospitals. And that's not medicine either, they're exterminating people left and right. First, they give them cancer with vaccines and then, they kill them with chemotherapy. That's the way things are done in the good old USA. There's no reason to use chemo, but they do anyway, despite the fact that it kills people 98% of the time within 5 years,[113] but it makes them money hand over fist, the cancer industry rakes in $200,000,000,000+ a year and that's far more important than human lives in this society.

> "Chemo and radiation are the top # 1 cancer causing treatments. Why would you treat cancer with a cancer-causing treatment?" - **Dr. Robert Morse, N.D**

Do you think they care about cures? That would put them out of business! Use your common sense! Chemotherapy is nitrogen mustard gas! It's the state's method of keeping the population down, it's not medicine! Can any oncologists please provide me with a list of people that you've cured with that stuff? How many, doc? Hmm? And if you're an oncologist I have another question; how do you sleep at night? Everyone you "treat" dies! How does it feel to murder people for money? I could never, ever spend my lifetime here engaged in such destructive and immoral behavior, especially when it involves innocent people who need helped as opposed to murdered.

> "I've met one oncologist in my life who wouldn't be classified as a sociopath...they are willing to give chemicals to a person, knowing they won't help the person...knowing that it causes harm, collecting the money for it, and moving on to the next patient, and that by definition would make them sociopathic. No conscience, no remorse, yet giving them drugs they themselves would never take...I know there are exceptions but I've only ever met one, in 30 years...she was the only one with a conscience." - **Dr. Michael Farley**

Anyone who administers poison to their fellow humans is not a doctor, they're paid population control agents for the state. Google up Dr. Stanislaw Burzynski sometime; his cure rates are readily available on the internet and his record speaks volumes. Let's compare that to the cure rate of mainstream oncologists who use chemotherapy, shall we? Most oncologists deserve prison time for what they do, but they're rewarded with high paying careers instead.

---

[113] https://www.ncbi.nlm.nih.gov/pubmed/15630849

Doing the state's dirty work for them is a high paying career! How nice! You must feel so very good about yourselves doing such a fine service for humanity! Hitler put Jews in ovens. They do it differently here. They try to be underhanded about it here, but at the same time it's in plain view. Americans are conditioned like robots to passively accept poisons in their food, water and in their so-called medicines. Americans have been programmed to believe that it's OK to drink toxic cocktails full of chemicals combined with processed sugar, a drug more addictive than cocaine, not a food:

> "Sugar is eight times more addictive than cocaine. And what's interesting is while cocaine and heroin activate only one spot for pleasure in the brain, sugar lights up the brain like a pinball machine." - **Dr. Mark Hyman**

There is zero nutritional value in sugar, it is quite literally a poison to the human body, which makes it a drug, not a food![114] Combined with a long list of toxic chemicals. Hmm. Soda pop is a surefire recipe for cancer and death but people drink it like it's going out of style. Nobody gives a rat's ass, and nobody drinks water anymore either. When they do, it's fluoridated too. Yes, most of your bottled water has fluoride too. Check your brands! It's just like the movie *Idiocracy* where they use Gatorade to water the crops. All the crops are dying and the sheeple are getting pissed because the new president wants to switch back to water! That scenario is real and true, except that people are trying to water themselves with deadly toxic chemicals, instead of drinking water! And that's why 1 in 3 people are being diagnosed with cancer in this day and age. It's really pretty obvious, but nobody cares enough to see. They scoff, laugh and ignore because they're brainwashed, and then they drink and smoke, chug Gatorade and vaccinate their kids, eat at McDonalds and take unnecessary drugs from their fake doctors......ingesting toxins galore and not giving a shit, laughing at me because I stopped doing it all, as much as I can avoid anyway. They see me not smoking, not drinking, not using prescriptions, not drinking soda pop, etc. and then they call me a square or make jokes. Have fun with your cancer then, and remember what I said when you get the diagnosis. It won't be so funny then. And I really do hope that you won't submit to chemotherapy either, it'll put you six feet

---

[114] There are much safer ways to sweeten food! Stevia is one example, which is a safe and natural herb that harms nobody.

under! People will accuse me of self-righteousness and tell me to step down off of my high-horse for this, but I'm not putting myself on any pedestals here, I'm simply telling it like it is. I used to engage in the same behavior (smoking, drinking, drugs, etc.) and I learned my lesson, but I'm not better than anybody. Cigarette smokers know how hazardous smoking is, but they keep puffing away. That's called self-abuse. These Americans are insane, they'll make up a long list of excuses; one of the more common ones is this:

"I'll just get hit by a truck if I stop smoking, or I'll die of something else entirely."

That is not logical! Self-neglect is acceptable for most Americans because "we all gotta go sometime." Americans don't even respect themselves or their own lives. Let's abuse ourselves into early graves, we're gonna die anyway! Who gives a shit, right Americans? The concept of taking care of themselves isn't allowed, poisoning themselves is the only option, they absolutely insist upon making that happen. That's not living, that's slow suicide. We came here to live not to die slowly at our own hands. Death is a part of it, yes. It's the end. But the end doesn't have to come so soon for most of us and our quality of life doesn't have to suck either, especially towards the end like it does for most of us because we can be in good health and enjoy life if we make that choice and take proper action! I certainly do feel way better compared to the way that I felt before I gave up the toxins! I have more energy, less brain fog, etc. and my quality of life has increased tenfold! "No one here gets out alive" is a true statement, but if your lifestyle is a deathstyle you need to wake up and smell the coffee. Killing yourself slowly isn't living, it's dying. As most Americans sit around waiting for the end to come, they miss out on the very reason that they came to this place; life.

Everything is loaded up heavily with chemicals in this society and nobody says a word about it! Nobody gives a shit! Even skin lotions, female makeup products, soaps, shampoos, etc. Do those chemicals have to be there? Yes or no? Are they necessary? I want to know what the purpose is then! Why is that stuff in there then? **<u>I demand a valid explanation</u>**. This is a great free country, right? So why does everything we consume contain poison that was officially put there by the US government then? What's your logical and rational excuse? I'm sure there is one, right? So why does your government poison you with everything they give you? Nobody seems to notice and nobody seems to care that the government wants us all dead. The science doesn't lie on this point either. There are clearly poisonous substances in our food, air, water, etc. It's not a false claim, it's undeniable. The piece that I'll be presenting below is not a proven fact and I don't claim it to be. Despite the source being unknown, this contains relevant information concerning the state that things are in today. Read along and you'll see how it relates to the medical system's poisons and most of the additional poisons in society, and describes the situation with precision accuracy. We might not know the source of this, but what it describes is exactly what they're doing. This piece puts the truth in the forefront, it points out what's happening. And I think that it will help people realize just how toxic this whole society really is. Read it and see. Supposedly this came from someone towards the top of the pyramid in the Illuminati and Freemasonry, a whistle blower, someone with a very troubled conscience trying to warn us, but the source isn't verified.[115]

<u>The Secret Covenant of the Illuminati</u>

"We will use our knowledge of science and technology in subtle ways so they will never see what is happening. We will use soft metals, aging accelerators and sedatives in food and water, also in the air. They will be blanketed by poisons everywhere they turn. The soft metals will cause them to lose their minds. We will promise to find a cure from our many fronts, yet we will feed them more poison. The poisons will be absorbed through their skin and mouths, they will destroy their minds and reproductive systems. From all this, their children will be born dead, and we will conceal this information. The poisons will be hidden in everything that surrounds them, in what they drink, eat, breathe and wear. We must be ingenious in dispensing the poisons for they can see far. We will teach them that the poisons are good, with fun images and musical tones. Those they look up to will help. We will enlist them to push our poisons. They will see our products being used in film and will grow accustomed to them and will never know their true effect. When they give birth we will inject poisons into the blood of their children and convince themit's for their help. We will start early on, when their minds are young, we will target their children with what children love most, sweet things. When their teeth decay we will fill them with metals that will kill their mind and steal their future. When their ability to learn has been affected, we will create medicine that will make them sicker and cause other diseases for which we will create yet more medicine. We will render them docile and weak before us by our power. They will grow depressed, slow and obese, and when they come to us for help, we will give them more poison. We will focus their attention toward money and material goods so they many never connect with their inner self. We will distract them with fornication, external pleasures and games so they may never be one with the oneness of it all. Their minds will belong to us and they will do as we say. If they refuse we shall find ways to implement mind-altering technology into their lives. We will use fear as our weapon. We will establish their governments and establish opposites within. We will own both sides. We will always hide our objective but carry out our plan. They will perform the labor for us and we shall prosper from their toil. Our families will never mix with theirs. Our blood must be pure always, for it is the way. We will make them kill each other when it suits us. We will keep

---

[115] https://www.infowars.com/the-secret-covenant-the-elites-manual-for-global-enslavement/

them separated from the oneness by dogma and religion. We will control all aspects of their lives and tell them what to think and how. We will guide them kindly and gently letting them think they are guiding themselves. We will foment animosity between them through our factions. When a light shall shine among them, we shall extinguish it by ridicule, or death, whichever suits us best. We will make them rip each other's hearts apart and kill their own children. We will accomplish this by using hate as our ally, anger as our friend. The hate will blind them totally, and never shall they see that from their conflicts we emerge as their rulers. They will be busy killing each other. They will bathe in their own blood and kill their neighbors for as long as we see fit. We will benefit greatly from this, for they will not see us, for they cannot see us. We will continue to prosper from their wars and their deaths. We shall repeat this over and over until our ultimate goal is accomplished. We will continue to make them live in fear and anger though images and sounds. We will use all the tools we have to accomplish this. The tools will be provided by their labor. We will make them hate themselves and their neighbors. We will always hide the divine truth from them, that we are all one. This they must never know! They must never know that a man's color is an illusion; they must always think they are not equal. Drop by drop, drop by drop we will advance our goal. We will take over their land, resources and wealth to exercise total control over them. We will deceive them into accepting laws that will steal the little freedom they will have. We will establish a money system that will imprison them forever, keeping them and their children in debt. When they shall ban together, we shall accuse them of crimes and present a different story to the world for we shall own all the media. We will use our media to control the flow of information and their sentiment in our favor. When they shall rise up against us we will crush them like insects, for they are less than that. They will be helpless to do anything for they will have no weapons. We will recruit some of their own to carry out our plans, we will promise them eternal life, but eternal life they will never have for they are not of us. The recruits will be called "initiates" and will be indoctrinated to believe false rites of passage to higher realms. Members of these groups will think they are one with us never knowing the truth. They must never learn this truth for they will turn against us. For their work they will be rewarded with earthly things and great titles, but never will they become immortal and join us, never will they receive the light and travel the stars. They will never reach the higher realms, for the killing of their own kind will prevent passage to the realm of enlightenment. This they will never know. The truth will be hidden in their face, so close they will not be able to focus on it until it's too late. Oh yes, so grand the illusion of freedom will be, that they will never know they are our slaves. When all is in place, the reality we will have created for them will own them. This reality will be their prison. They will live in self-delusion. When our goal is accomplished a new era of domination will begin. Their minds will be bound by their beliefs, the beliefs we have established from time immemorial. But if they ever find out they are our equal, we shall perish then. THIS THEY MUST NEVER KNOW. If they ever find out that together they can vanquish us, they will take action. They must never, ever find out what we have done, for if they do, we shall have no place to run, for it will be easy to see who we are once the veil has fallen. Our actions will have revealed who we are and they will hunt us down and no person shall give us shelter. This is the secret covenant by which we shall live the rest of our present and future lives, for this reality will transcend many generations and life spans. This covenant is sealed by blood, our blood. We are the ones who from heaven to earth came. This covenant must NEVER, EVER be known to exist. It must NEVER, EVER be written or spoken of for if it is, the consciousness it will spawn will release the fury of the PRIME CREATOR upon us and we shall be cast to the depths from whence we came and remain there until the end time of infinity itself." - **Author Unknown**

Again, this isn't officially verified. I don't claim it as solid evidence, it's only circumstantial, but I feel it describes in detail what they're doing in this society, and my intuition tells me it's authentic. You decide, yourself, I make no claims on that one although there is no denying that biological warfare is in fact being used against the population and has been for decades plus.

> **Biological Warfare: adjective** 1. The use of a biological toxin or infectious agents such as chemicals, bacteria, viruses and fungi, with intent to kill or cause disease and/or biological harm.

But what is in fact verified is that they, the elite higher-ups in our world's governments, worship Moloch, an owl deity, in a Satanic ritual called "The Cremation of Care" at secret meetings of the Illuminati at Bohemian Grove in California once per year. This has become public knowledge even the mainstream has picked it up. [116] Alex Jones snuck himself in and filmed it [117] and it's on *YouTube* therefore very hard to deny. Listen to the video of the ceremony and keep in mind that these are your Presidents and World Leaders. I can't just ignore this like everyone else! **This is not one bit OK with me!**

"Moloch was one of many pagan gods worshiped by means of human sacrifice. Pagans who worshiped Moloch often sacrificed one of their own children, who was ritually murdered and then placed in a sacrificial altar of fire. The sacrifice of the child was to assure a blessing of prosperity for the family. Some followed the Canaanite practice of placing under the front doorstep of the family home, the bones that remained after the burning of the child. In short, a child was murdered for the promised convenience and prosperity the family was to receive from Moloch."[118]

---

[116] https://www.washingtonpost.com/blogs/blogpost/post/bohemian-grove-where-the-rich-and-powerful-go-to-misbehave/2011/06/15/AGPV1sVH_blog.html?utm_term=.da89ccdade84

[117] https://www.youtube.com/watch?v=r5dHhvpHIjM&t=6s

[118] http://www.religiousfreedomcoalition.org/2011/01/21/worshiping-moloch-%E2%80%93-the-human-sacrifice-of-children-to-assure-prosperity/

Ronald Reagan and Richard Nixon sitting at Bohemian Grove together in 1967, long before either one of them had become President.

This ritual goes back thousands of years. The Bohemian Club's all-male membership features Presidents, government officials, artists, musicians, cabinet officials, CEOs of large corporations including major financial institutions, major military contractors, oil companies, banks including the Federal Reserve and utilities including nuclear power.

> "Satanism has pervaded western civilization ...It has been growing for thousands of years, quietly weaving its way through the very fabric of the culture and the power structures of the nations in the West. It has adherents in all walks of life, in all incomes, and all social strata. It has exerted a profound influence on the intellectual life of the West for the past several hundred years ...Satanism has influenced politics, economics, art and music, through the spiritual-psychological process called dissociation, and dissociation is as old as human culture itself." - **Phillip Eugene de Rothschild**

Many believe that plotting and planning took place at Bohemian Grove for the creation and eventual use of the atomic bomb. It is most certainly undeniable that the use of the bomb against Japan was unnecessary[119] and that the excuses given to us in our "history" classes were lies. The Lucifer worshipers were looking for an excuse to drop their bombs. General Dwight D. Eisenhower had urged them not to use the atomic bomb. After the war ended, he had this to say:

> "It wasn't necessary to hit them with that awful thing." - **Gen. Dwight D. Eisenhower**

Truman's Chief of Staff, William D. Leahy, said in his diary that he thought the war could have ended on acceptable terms during June of 1945. He also said:

---

[119] https://www.nytimes.com/1988/10/29/opinion/l-a-bombing-of-japan-was-unnecessary-393488.html

"...the use of this barbarous weapon at Hiroshima and Nagasaki was of no material assistance in our war against Japan. The Japanese were already defeated and ready to surrender. In being the first to use it, we adopted an ethical standard common to the barbarians of the Dark Ages."

Fritz Springmeier, author of *The Bloodlines of the Illuminati* states that the Illuminati at the highest levels consists of 13 main families; Astor, Bundy, Collins, Dupont, Freeman, Kennedy, Li, Onassis, Rockefeller, Rothschild, Russell, Van Duhn and Merovingian. They interbreed as much as possible to keep the royal bloodlines pure, hence the arranged marriages; Charles and Diana, Hillary and Bill, Jackie and JFK, etc. They are all members of secret societies such as the Illuminati, Freemasons, Bilderberg Group, Knights of Malta, Knights Templar, Cathars, Skull and Bones, Priory of Sion, Rosicrucians, Assassins and others. Every President in US history, bar one, was directly bloodline descended from King John of England! America was founded by British monarchs of the Bavarian Illuminati and Freemasonry.

"The remarkable discovery was made by 12-year-old BridgeAnne d'Avignon, of Salinas, California, who created a ground-breaking family tree that connected **42 of 43** U.S. presidents to one common, and rather unexpected, ancestor: **King John of England**."[120]

Trump and the Clintons are long-time friends and business associates.

"Donald and Hillary are **19th cousins**...genealogy experts say (they)...**share a common ancestor from England 18 generations ago**. The common ancestors are John of Gaunt, the duke of Lancaster, and third wife Katherine Swynford at the end of the 14th century — a century before Columbus sailed the ocean blue. One of their children was Joan Beaufort, whose descendants include Mrs. Clinton. Her brother John Beaufort is an ancestor of Mr. Trump. Their descendants included **several kings of England** and centuries of Scottish kings. 'Their 19th great grandfather is King Edward III [**John's father**] so there is precedent for ruling a country, **it's in their genes**,' A.J. Jacobs said."[121] (emphasis my own)

---

[120] http://www.dailymail.co.uk/news/article-2183858/All-presidents-bar-directly-descended-medieval-English-king.html

[121] https://www.washingtontimes.com/news/2015/aug/25/donald-trump-hillary-clinton-are-related-genealogy/

Nice, huh? This "country" is not a country at all, it's still a part of Britain, a British Crown colony, a Virginia corporation.[122] *Google* "USA INC BIN # 28 USC 3002 Section 15" and see for yourself! They manufactured this place as an experimental mind-controlled prison society complete with fake and staged independence from their headquarters in Britain, the Vatican and later Israel. These secret societies run the world via the Rothschild central banks. The Federal Reserve is not a federal entity it is a private bank and private banks control all of America's money, as they do almost every other country on the planet except for a few.

"...there is a power so organized, so subtle, so complete, so pervasive, that they had better not speak above their breath when they speak in condemnation of it."- **Woodrow Wilson, 28th President**

"Author and lecturer **David Wilcock** outlined a plan that 'has been meticulously followed for at least 300 years. The economic, political and social concerns we struggle with today are the result of a plan that was systematically put into practice as of 1776 with the founding of the Order of the Illuminati in Bavaria. This group networked, infiltrated, consolidated and enacted plans that had been in place for much longer periods of time. They created the hidden infrastructure, secrecy, membership, documentation and blueprints necessary to effectuate what they had hoped would be a global takeover—in the hopes of declaring a New World Order.' Wilcock said for many years he has had hundreds of dreams in which he sees **a 'massive, unprecedented exposure and arrest of this cabal on a worldwide level**...this will indeed be of tremendous, unprecedented, positive benefit to humanity.'"[123]

---

[122] https://www.bibliotecapleyades.net/sociopolitica/sociopol_globalbanking92.htm

[123] As quoted from pages 308-309 of *The Illuminati: The Secret Society That Hijacked the World* by Jim Marrs

Why would the elite so commonly use Satanic symbols, especially out in public the way they do? They aren't rock stars, they're politicians! This isn't Ozzy Osbourne and he's not at an Iron Maiden concert! This is the Vice President of the United States of America and he's at the Republican National Convention. Why do they do this goat-head symbol so much? And what's up with Bohemian Grove? Hmm? Go ahead, call me crazy.

Despite Skull and Bones being a very small elite brotherhood from Yale with a very small membership list consisting of less than ½ of 1% of the population, in 2004 we had two candidates running for President who were both in Skull and Bones; George W. Bush and John Kerry.[124] Take a look at the video footage of their initiation ceremony.[125] Their rituals and ceremonies include nice things such as lying nude in a coffin and revealing their sexual secrets to other members while they simultaneously masturbate, blood oaths of allegiance, white supremacy, drinking blood from a human skull,[126] and other things perfectly suitable for children's parties. Nice election huh? Take your pick, no such thing as the lesser of two evils in this case!

> "If you vote you have no right to complain. Now, some people like to twist that around. They say 'If you don't vote you have no right to complain,' but where's the logic in that? If you vote, and you elect dishonest, incompetent politicians, and they get into office and screw everything up, you are responsible for what they have done. You voted them in. You caused the problem. You have no right to complain." - **George Carlin**

Take note of John Kerry's continued prominent status in high level government. He knew he was going to lose their staged election! They arrange all Presidents long in advance according to royal bloodlines, it's a hoax, not a real country. The Rothschild family has the most control; they own and control Israel, America, the EU, Africa, et al as seen above, and along with the Queen and the Pope, they run their New World Order from three city-states, or independent countries, which all form what is known as *The Empire of the City*.

---

¹²⁴ https://www.bibliotecapleyades.net/sociopolitica/esp_sociopol_skullbones03.htm

¹²⁵ https://www.youtube.com/watch?v=DD-JttocUzk

¹²⁶ http://www.booboone.com/skull-and-bones-secret-society/

Vatican = religious control
Washington D.C. = military control
London = economic control.[127]

David Rockefeller, Pope Benedict XVI, Jacob Rothschild, Prince Phillip, Queen Elizabeth, Pope Francis

---

[127] https://www.bibliotecapleyades.net/sociopolitica/esp_sociopol_911_68.htm

Pedophilia runs rampant in the Roman Catholic Church.

The reason there is a lot of unreported child trafficking in D.C., the Vatican and UK is because these Satanists engage in child sacrifice for their rituals. They also grow and harvest children before they become documented and use them that way, holding women hostage for that specific purpose. Pedophilia runs rampant, which is public knowledge concerning the Roman Catholic Church.[128] And the Pope always defends the molesters[129] but for the most part, these child trafficking rings go under-reported or not reported at all in your fine free press.[130] The British Royal family is involved too, of course, and reports are *plenty* concerning their ritualistic Satanic abuse, child trafficking, pedophilia and involvement in everything that goes on behind the scenes.[131]

---

[128] http://nationalpost.com/holy-post/pope-francis-says-about-8000-pedophiles-are-members-of-catholic-clergy-including-bishops-and-cardinals

[129] http://www.independent.co.uk/news/world/australasia/pope-francis-paedophile-priests-backsliding-francis-sullivan-australia-a7625231.html

[130] http://www.collective-evolution.com/2017/03/31/nbc-news-report-hillary-clinton-covered-up-pedophile-ring-at-state-department/

[131] http://beforeitsnews.com/power-elite/2015/06/about-the-satanic-pedophile-practices-of-the-english-royal-family-2449150.html

Did you ever stop to think about the fact that these people never lift a finger to feed the starving children or help the poor at all? The Queen is worth **trillions**! So is the Vatican. They could solve poverty overnight if they so desired. To the Pope and the Catholic Church: **"You're doing it wrong! Jesus would want those children fed, clothed and housed, not left to suffer!"** Lucifer is their God. Not Jesus.

I don't think the Pope is an Iron Maiden fan either, so what's up with the goat-head symbol of Satan then? And why does his church molest children so much? The Pope that mysteriously died in office after 33 days, Pope John Paul I, was in fact trying to remove Freemasons from the church. He didn't want that in his church because he knew who they are and what they're up to. He was found poisoned.[132] Most of the men at the top of the pyramid at the Vatican and in the Mormon church and others are also in the Illuminati at the highest levels. Mormonism is basically Freemasonry in disguise.[133] Almost all higher-level Freemasons (31st, 32nd and 33rd degrees) are also in the Illuminati.[134] Most of the higher-ups in the corporate world are Illuminati. The Illuminati recruits high-profile people, like Bono from U2 for example, to join their little club and that's why you were seeing Bono hanging out with George Bush and several other high-profile elites quite often in the press in recent decades.[135] Bill Gates was recruited as well. The Illuminati even have their very own website! Look what they say about Bill Gates!

---

[132] http://www.cai.org/bible-studies/pope-was-poisoned-after-33-days

[133] https://en.wikipedia.org/wiki/Mormonism_and_Freemasonry

[134] Details in *The Illuminati: The Secret Society That Hijacked The World* by Jim Marrs

[135] http://www.hangthebankers.com/bono-exposed-as-a-complete-fraud/

"The Illuminati supports the positive efforts of this planet's elite and the initiative of the Giving Pledge. Originally conceived by Bill and Melinda Gates and Warren Buffett, the Giving Pledge encourages those with much to consider the needs of those with less."[136]

Basic Illuminati Pyramid Structure

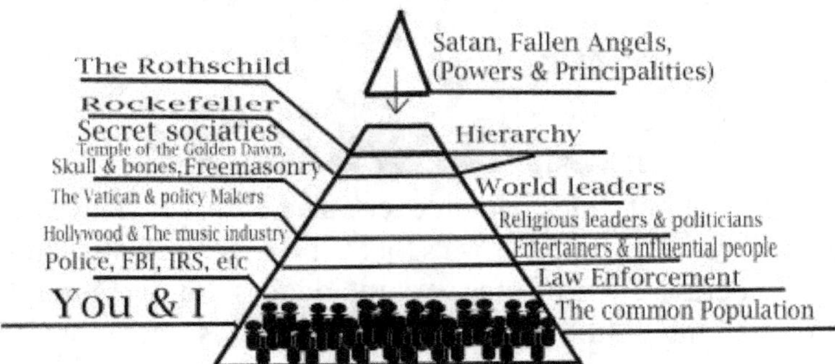

911 was portrayed on the Simpsons four years in advance.

Hollywood is run by the Illuminati as well. They put mind-control in your movies. They showed 911 on the Simpsons four years before it ever happened. Is that coincidental? No.

---

[136] https://www.illuminatiofficial.org/billionaire-giving-pledge/

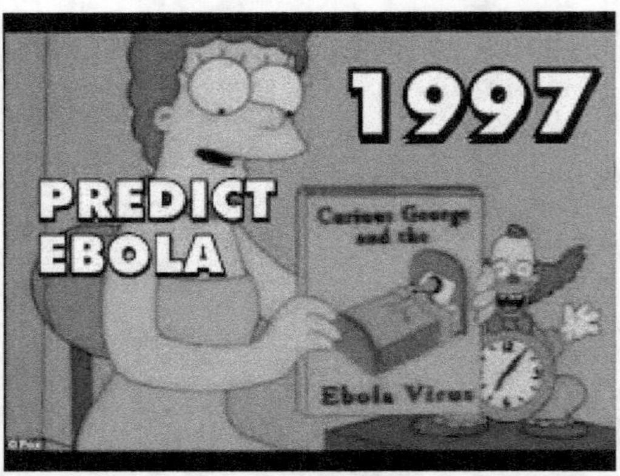

How about this? Coincidence? The episode where the Ebola book appeared was called "Lisa's Sax" and first aired on October 19, 1997.[137] There are ten of these "coincidences" on the Simpsons.[138] They're playing with your heads! Here are some more various examples:

The Illuminati letting you know what you need to ask about if you desire to learn the truth: "ASK ABOUT ILLUMINATI."

---

[137] http://www.dailymail.co.uk/news/article-2786966/How-The-Simpsons-predicted-US-Ebola-outbreak-1997-Episode-shows-Marge-offering-sick-Bart-children-s-book-Curious-George-Ebola-Virus.html

[138] https://www.thesun.co.uk/living/2149067/what-else-did-the-simpsons-call-first-here-are-10-eerie-predictions-on-the-show-that-came-true/

Trade-Center-Defender
SCORE: 0
EARLY 2001   TRADE CENTER DEFENDER

1994

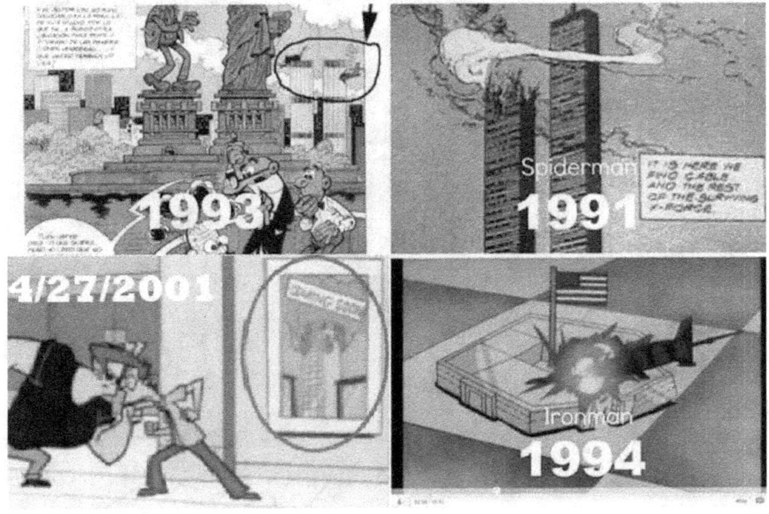
1993
Spiderman
1991
IT IS HERE WE
FIND CABLE
AND THE REST
OF THE SURVIVING
X-FORCE
4/27/2001
Ironman
1994

The pictures below are from a card game that came out in 1995. He started producing it in 1990.

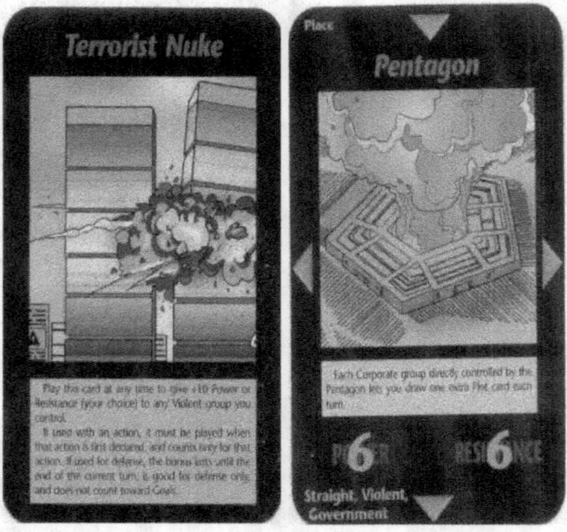

"In 1990, role-playing inventor, Steve Jackson, was planning his newest game, which he would ultimately call *'Illuminati -New World Order'* Game the *'Illuminati — New World Order'* Game, or 'INWO' for short is played with a deck of special cards, money chips (representing millions of dollars in low-nominal unmarked banknotes) and two six-sided dice. The players take role of Illuminati societies that struggle to take over the world. The Pocket Box edition depicted six Illuminati groups: The Bavarian Illuminati, The Discordian Society, The UFOs, The Servants of Cthulhu, The Bermuda Triangle, and The Gnomes of Zürich. The deluxe edition added the Society of Assassins and The Network, and the Illuminati Y2K expansion added the Church of The SubGenius and Shangri-La."

Predicted 2010 BP Oil spill

There are many more examples of 911, just go to *Google* and look it up. This is all easily explained. The bottom line is this; this whole place is a staged, rigged game. It's a con. Your news is fake, your history is fake, your wars are staged, your terror attacks are staged, your elections are rigged, your medicine is fake (designed to kill you), your food is fake (designed to give you cancer and disease), your education is fake (designed to hold up the status-quo by indoctrinating human robots), your science is fake (designed to promote their agenda), and on and on...even this country's supposed independence from Britain is staged fraud, it's fake too![139] All the world truly is a stage, and one set of families who worship Moloch in the woods and pay homage to Lucifer are pulling the strings. You've been lied to all your lives. Christians are adamant that Lucifer is all about deception. We've all clearly been deceived. Only it's a little bit different than what Christians thought. Christians have been unknowingly cheering for Lucifer the entire time, and proudly sending their children to die in wars for Lucifer. Your great Christian nation was founded by Lucifer in the first place. Whether you take that literally or not is up to you, but "Lucifer" is in fact a representation of the dark forces in control of the planet Earth at this time via these secret brotherhoods because they worship Lucifer as their God and have since the beginning.

The very first third party that was ever established in the USA was the Anti-Masonic Party founded by Henry Dana Ward, Thurlow Reed and William H. Seward in the year 1829. Resistance to the agenda of Freemasons and Illuminati goes all the way back in history.

One thing that is giving the people some power now is the age of information. We have more knowledge and info at our disposal now than ever before, thanks to the Illuminati putting the internet up for us! And yes, they did that too! Any technology that you see out in society is a mere one tenth or less of what they have tucked away out of view, in their labs. Don't think for a second that what you see is all there is! They give you toys to keep you entertained, but the real technology is hidden! Only the people at the top of the pyramid know what's going on worldwide with the banking families and the Illuminati, the rest of the people, including many in government, are in the dark. They think it's a real country. It's not. It's a rigged game. A mind-control experiment set up by the Illuminati. America is only one of their experiments; they own and control most other countries as well. Keep in mind that one power

---

[139] https://www.bibliotecapleyades.net/sociopolitica/sociopol_globalbanking92.htm

has been staging your history by funding all sides simultaneously. The French Revolution was a Masonic movement,[140] Wall Street funded the Bolshevik Revolution,[141] and the Rothschild family funded both sides of the American Civil War!

> "The Civil War was planned in London by Rothschild who wanted two American democracies, each burdened with debt. Four years before the war (1857) Rothschild decided his Paris bank would support the South, represented by Sen. John Slidell, from Louisiana; while the British branch would support the North, represented by August Belmont (Schoenberg), from New York. The plan was to bankroll, at usurious interest rates, the huge war debts that were anticipated, using that debt to extort both sides into accepting a Rothschild central bank."[142]

Even the Boston Tea Party was staged by Freemasons![143]

> "One of the most influential figures in the American Revolution was the writer, philosopher and scientist Benjamin Franklin. In February 1731, he became a Rosicrucian Mason and in 1734 Provincial Grand Master of Pennsylvania. While in France in the 1770's, as a diplomat for the American colonies, Franklin was made Grand Master of the politically-oriented Masonic lodge called Neuf Soeurs in Paris."[144]

It's all a lie, every last bit of it:

> "It's ALL Bollocks. Yes, ALL of it." - **David Icke**

You've been mind-controlled all your life and now you get to read the words of truth. There are more and more people like myself now who are fed information from the light. I am open, honest and I have a strong desire to know the truth behind the lies, therefore I attract that to myself. I attract key information to myself that most people never see. It's because I am working for the light with the firm intentions of doing good with the knowledge that I seek, and as far as I'm concerned one of the best ways to combat the evil forces in charge is to expose their game for all to see. That's why I write these books and do things to educate others, and that's why I engage in research. Knowledge is power. Silence is consent.

In Washington D.C. there stands a statue of a man named Albert Pike, who was a Captain for the Confederates during the Civil War, the founder of the Ku Klux Klan as well as a 33rd degree Freemason and a high-ranking member of the Illuminati. There have

---

[140] https://dr-david-harrison.com/papers-articles-and-essays/freemasonry-and-the-french-revolution/

[141] https://www.amazon.com/Wall-Street-Bolshevik-Revolution-Capitalists/dp/190557035X

[142] http://abundanthope.net/pages/True_US_History_108/The-Civil-War-and-the-Role-of-the-Illuminati_printer.shtml

[143] http://www.traditionalcatholicpriest.com/2015/07/04/us-revolution-begins-by-masons-boston-tea-party/

[144] https://www.henrymakow.com/2015/11/America-Was-Founded-by-the-Illuminati%20.html

been protests to get that statue taken down due to the controversial nature of who he is and what he's said and done, but the government refuses to remove it. He is one of their all-time favorite Illuminists. He's their hero. Aside from the fact that he founded the KKK, he claimed to channel Lucifer as the Grand Master of the Order of the Palladium. Take a look at some of the things he's said publicly on record:

"That which we must say to the world is that we worship a god, but it is the god that one adores without superstition. To you, Sovereign Grand Inspectors General, we say this, that you may repeat it to the brethren of the 32nd, 31st and 30th degrees: The masonic Religion should be, by all of us initiates of the higher degrees, maintained in the Purity of the Luciferian doctrine. If Lucifer were not God, would Adonay and his priests calumniate him? Yes, Lucifer is God... thus, the doctrine of Satanism is a heresy,   and the true and pure philosophical religion is the belief in Lucifer, the equal of Adonay; but Lucifer, God of Light and God of Good, is struggling for humanity against Adonay, the God of Darkness and Evil."

As a matter of fact, Freemasons and the Bavarian Illuminati founded America. The Illuminati was founded (by Adam Weishaupt) the very same year that America was founded, 1776[145] and was financed by the Nathan Rothschild controlled bank of England. Sheer coincidence, right? Not at all. Don't forget that every US President, bar one, was directly bloodline descended from King John of England! Weishaupt took the Rothschild funding and infiltrated Freemasonry in order to cloak the Illuminati's activities.

---

[145] https://en.wikipedia.org/wiki/Illuminati

"In secrecy our strength principally lies. On this account we should always conceal ourselves under the name of some other association. The inferior lodges of Free Masonry are the most convenient cloaks for our grand object, because the world is already familiarized with the idea that nothing of importance, or worthy of attention can spring from Masonry."

"The great strength of our Order lies in its concealment; let it never appear in any place in its own name, but always concealed by another name, and another occupation. None is fitter than the lower degrees of Freemasonry; the public is accustomed to it, expects little from it, and therefore takes little notice of it. Next to this, the form of a learned or literary society is best suited to our purpose, and had Freemasonry not existed, this cover would have been employed; and it may be much more than a cover, it may be a powerful engine in our hands. … A Literary Society is the most proper form for the introduction of our Order into any state where we are yet strangers."

"No man can give any account of the Order of Freemasonry, of its origin, of its history, of its objects, nor any explanation of its mysteries and symbols, which does not leave the mind in total uncertainty on all these points."

"Because the true purposes of Illuminism were so shocking, Weishaupt constantly encouraged the **secretive nature of the order**. No member was ever allowed himself to be identified an Illuminati. The words Illuminism or Illuminati were never to be used in correspondence, but were to be replaced by the astrological symbol for the sun, a circle with a dot in the middle." - **William T. Still** [146] (emphasis my own)

---

[146] *New World Order: The Ancient Plan of Secret Societies* by William T. Still

Just about every founder was high up in Freemasonry, which would make them Illuminati as well.[147] In response to a letter warning him about the Illuminati operating in America, George Washington said:

> "It was not my intention to doubt that the Doctrines of the Illuminati and the principles of Jacobinism had not spread into the United States. On the contrary, **no one is more truly satisfied of this fact than I am**." (emphasis my own)

Fifty-five of fifty-six signatories on the Declaration of Independence were known Freemasons.[148] George Washington has a masonic memorial near D.C. as well. [149] The Supreme Headquarters of the 33rd degree of the Scottish Rite of Freemasonry is located near the White House at 1733 16th St.

"When the Grand Master Freemason, George Washington, became the first President, he nominated eleven Supreme Court Justices, at least six of which were confirmed Freemasons. The same story has continued ever since. The inauguration of Washington in 1789 was a Freemasonic ceremony in which he swore the oath on a Freemasonic Bible. In January 2001 President George W. Bush took the oath using that same Bible, as did his father more than a decade earlier. It is the property of the New York Lodge, according to news reports. Washington, who commanded the American colonial armies against the British Crown, was a Knight of the Order of the Garter, one of the most `elite Illuminati networks headed by the British Crown!" - **David Icke**[150]

---

[147] https://www.usnews.com/opinion/articles/2009/09/14/masons-and-the-making-of-america

[148] *The Illuminati: The Secret Society That Hijacked the World* by Jim Marrs

[149] https://gwmemorial.org/

[150] *Children of the Matrix: How An Interdimensional Race Has Controlled the World for Thousands of Years and Still Does* by David Icke

Washington   Baphomet

The statue above is on display at the *Smithsonian Museum of American History*. Note the nearly identical pose; half-naked from the waist up, wearing a toga, the right arm up and the left arm down.

And here we have Uncle Sam as compared to Baphomet. Note the star in the forehead area, the goatee, the identical stare and angry expression.

A Masonic apron made in France and presented to George Washington at Mount Vernon in 1784 by Marquis de Lafayette, a former general and close friend of Washington's, who was also a Freemason.

Concerning Washington's apron above; pay special attention to the beehive at the very top as it is an ancient symbol of the mystery schools and secret societies dating all the way back to the Brotherhood of the Snake and ancient Sumer. Joseph Smith, Brigham Young and all successive Mormon church leaders were and are high level Freemasons and Illuminati members as well.

"The symbol is a very ancient one... The bee was used as a symbol in ancient Egypt, and the beehive symbol dates back to at least ancient Rome. The beehive as a symbol was adopted by many Friendly Societies, Trade Unions and insurance companies, the hive representing Beehive industry and the bees the workers. The Roman writer Porphyry, in his work De antro nympharum (The Cave of the Nymphs), tells us that in the Roman rites of Mithra, honey from a honeycomb was poured over the initiate during the Leo (Lion) ritual while he was admonished to avoid all that which is unclean in the world. The Church of the Latter Day Saints also adopted the symbol and it may be featured in the Book of Mormon, when it states that the Jaredites carried "with them Deseret, which, by interpretation, is a honey bee" (Ether 2:3)." - **Dr. David Harrison**[151]

As for the All-Seeing-Eye of the Illuminati:

"As one Masonic book says, 'These considerations lead us to an interesting topic, the Eye of Mind or the Eye of Horus ... and conveying the idea of the 'All seeing Eye'. The end set before the Egyptian neophyte was illumination, that is to be 'brought to light'. The Religion of Egypt was the Religion of the Light".[152]

---

[151] https://dr-david-harrison.com/freemasonry/the-lost-symbols-of-freemasonry-the-beehive/

[152] *The Symbolism of the Gods of the Egyptians and the Light They Throw on Freemasonry* by Thomas Milton Stewart

"The Light to which Masons constantly refer, and toward which they are to constantly move, is the Religion of Horus! This is damning, because in Egyptian Mythology, Horus IS Lucifer."

"The Latin name Lucifer is an exact translation of the Greek term Phōsphoros., which stems from Horus (Phosp*Horus*), a name meaning 'Light-Bringer', is the 'Morning Star', the planet Venus. The 'Vulgate' (Latin translation of the Bible) translates Hebrew 'Helel' (Venus as the brilliant, bright or shining one) to 'Lucifer' understandably."[153]

"Many proposed designs were submitted for a flag for the new Confederacy. The above proposal, which is preserved today in the *United States National Archives*, prominently feature the Brotherhood's symbol of the All-Seeing-Eye. The Confederate leaders eventually opted for a simple cross bars and stars design." - **William Bramley**[154]

And in the ancient Pyramid texts of Egypt we see the following concerning Horus:

"The reed-floats of the sky are set in place for me, that I may cross by means of them to Ra at the horizon. ...I will stand among them, for the moon is my brother, the Morning Star is my offspring..."

The Egyptian hieroglyph for the morning star literally translates to "divine knowledge" [155] which is what these secret societies and mystery schools are all about, esoteric or divine wisdom and/or hidden knowledge.

"Jefferson, the writer of the Declaration of Independence, was responsible for infiltrating the Illuminati into the newly organized lodges of the 'Scottish Rite' in New England. Jefferson defended Weishaupt (the Bavarian Illuminati's founder) saying: 'As Weishaupt lived under the tyranny of a despot and priests, he knew that caution was necessary even in spreading information, and the principles of pure morality. This has given an air of mystery to his views, was the foundation of his banishment... If Weishaupt had written here, where no secrecy is necessary in our endeavors to render men wise and virtuous, he would not have thought of any secret machinery for that purpose.'"[156]

---

[153] https://en.wikipedia.org/wiki/Phosphorus_%28morning_star%29

[154] *The Gods of Eden* by William Bramley

[155] *The Hiram Key: Pharaohs, Freemasonry, and the Discovery of the Secret Scrolls of Jesus* by Christopher Knight and Robert Lomas

[156] https://www.henrymakow.com/2015/11/America-Was-Founded-by-the-Illuminati%20.html

"Semiramis as the Statue of Liberty which was given to New York by French Freemasons in Paris who knew what the figure really symbolized - the goddess of Babylon."[157]

Lady Liberty originated in ancient Babylon with the goddess Semiramis whose son Nimrod was the famed founder of the city. Another Semiramis statue just like the one in New York resides in Paris on the River Seine.[158] The crown of thorns represents the rays of the sun. The torch of the Illuminated Ones represents the light or the way of Lucifer. It is the signature of theancient brotherhoods telling us in a symbolic way that they are in charge here.[159] The streets of D.C. are adorned with Freemasonic and Illuminati symbols and the architecture of the entire city is the work of Freemasons[160] In the streets we see a pentagram, a masonic compass and square, and the pyramid capstone (minus the All-Seeing-Eye), which is also their symbolism on the back of the dollar bill.

---

157 *Human Race Get Off Your Knees: The Lion Sleeps No More* by David Icke

158 *The Biggest Secret* by David Icke

159 *Tales from the Time Loop* by David Icke

160 *The Secret Architecture of Our Nation's Capital* by David Ovason

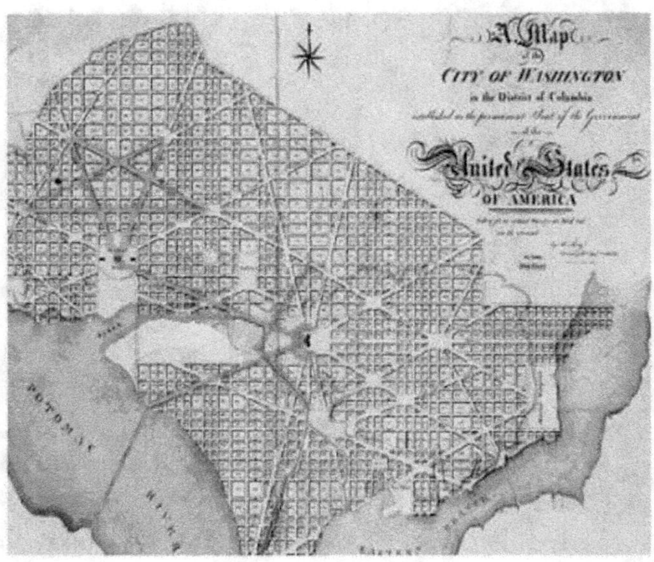

"The real rulers in Washington are invisible, and exercise power from behind the scenes." - *Supreme Court Justice* **Felix Frankfurter**, *1952*

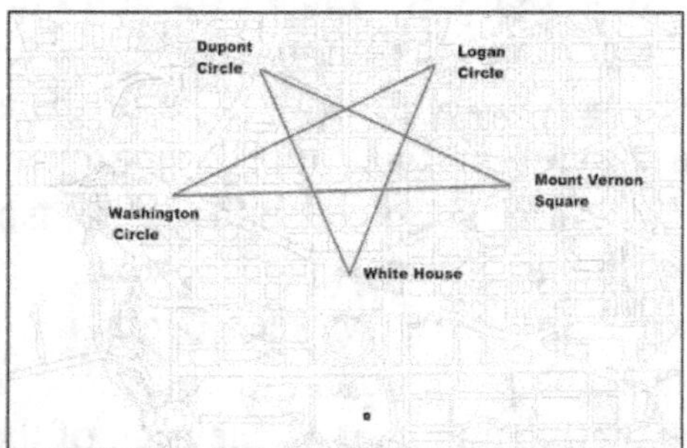

"The United States of America was chosen to lead the world into this...[New   World Order] from the beginning. In 1791, Pierre Charles L'Enfante (the designer who was a Freemason), laid out Governmental Center of Washington, D.C., he planned more than just streets, roads and buildings. He hid certain occultic magical symbols in the layout. When these symbols are united they become one large Luciferic or occultic, symbol. The upper four points of the Goathead represent the four elements of the world, Fire, Water, Earth and Air. The bottom fifth point represents the spirit of Lucifer. It demonstrates beyond the shadow of a doubt, that our leadership has been knowingly and consistently been pursuing a hidden agenda which, when fully carried out, will mean the destruction of our nation (the U.S.) as we know it today and the beginning of the... New World Order."[161]

---

[161] http://freemasonrywatch.org/washington.html

The city design features Freemasonic lodges and mystical and ritual sites, Pagan statues, busts and artwork, and much more. D.C. is a proverbial shrine to ancient ritualistic and occultic symbolism. The book *The Secrets of Masonic Washington: A Guidebook to the Signs, Symbols, and Ceremonies at the Origin of America's Capital* by James Wasserman takes you through a photographic tour of the city showing the many sites making the case quite clear.

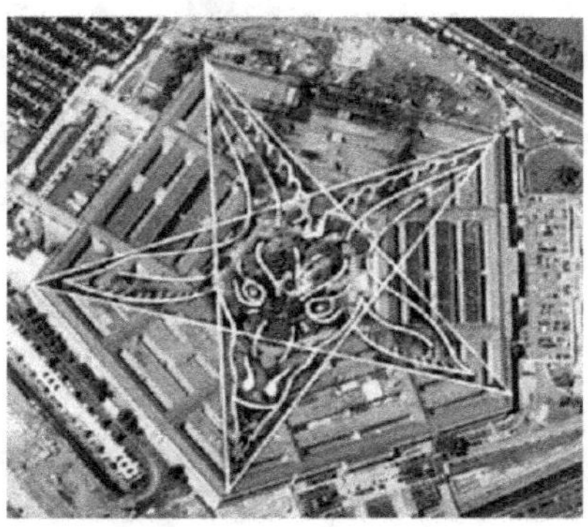

Don't forget that they have the *pentagon* as their war center!

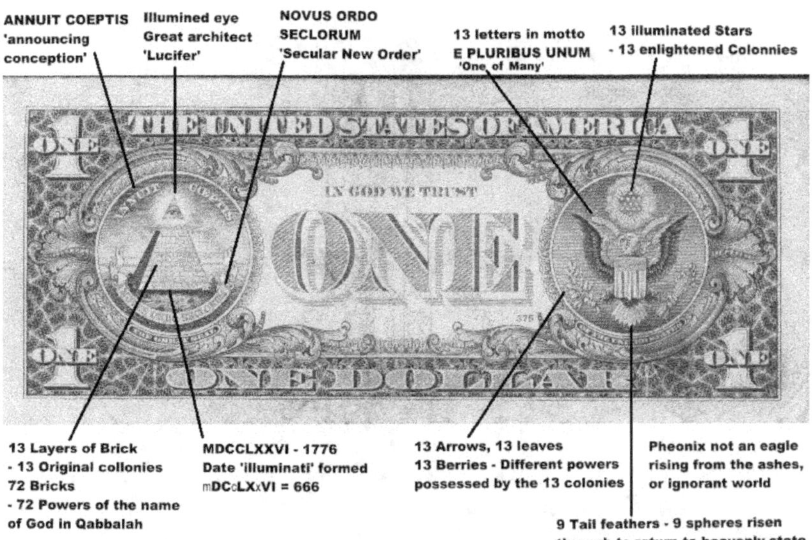

Look at the back of a dollar bill! [162] There have been Luciferian forces in power for as long as we've all been alive, they actually built America from the ground up! I had no idea about any

---

[162] *The Secret Symbols of the Dollar Bill* by David Ovason

of this stuff until about ten years ago. As open minded as I am it took me until I was into my 40's before I figured it out. Most people never do. They think it's a free country. It's not. It's a cage and we're rodents or cockroaches to them. Sheep in a pen! We're useful for them to get what they want from us and then they throw us away. The United States of America is a mind-controlled society under the helm of Satanists. It's been hidden in your face the whole time!

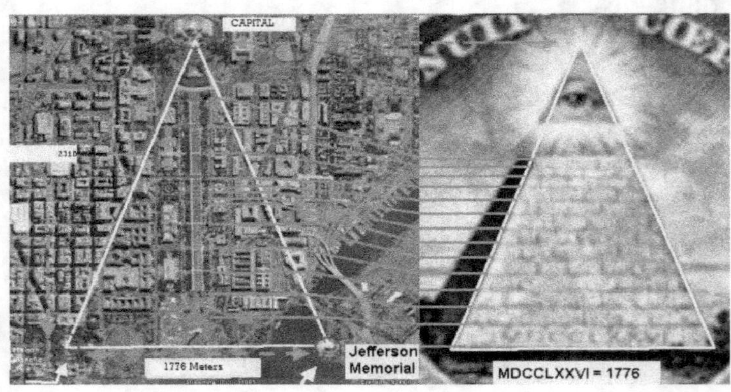

Take note of the "MASON" anagram above as well.

Albert Pike outlined the Illuminati's pre-planned and staged World Wars long in advance. In a letter to 33rd degree Freemason and Illuminati head, politician and Mafia founder Giuseppe Mazzini, dated August 15, 1871, Pike said the following:

"The First World War must be brought about in order to permit the Illuminati to overthrow the power of the Czars in Russia and of making that country a fortress of atheistic Communism. The divergences caused by the 'agentur' (agents) of the Illuminati between the British and Germanic Empires will be used to foment this war. At the end of the war, Communism will be built and used in order to destroy the other governments and in order to weaken the religions.

"The Second World War must be fomented by taking advantage of the differences between the Fascists and the political Zionists. This war must be brought about so that Nazism is destroyed and that the political Zionism be strong enough to institute a sovereign state of Israel in Palestine. During the Second World War, International Communism must become strong enough in order to balance Christendom, which would be then restrained and held in check until the time when we would need it for the final social cataclysm.

"The Third World War must be fomented by taking advantage of the differences caused by the 'agentur' of the 'Illuminati' between the political Zionists and the leaders of Islamic World. The war must be conducted in such a way that Islam (the Moslem Arabic World) and political Zionism (the State of Israel) mutually destroy each other. Meanwhile the other nations, once more divided on this issue will be constrained. physical, moral, spiritual and economical exhaustion…We shall unleash the Nihilists and the atheists, and we shall provoke a formidable social cataclysm which in all its horror will show clearly to the nations the effect of absolute atheism, origin of savagery and of the most bloody turmoil. Then everywhere, the citizens, obliged to defend themselves against the world minority of revolutionaries, will exterminate those destroyers of civilization, and the multitude, disillusioned with Christianity, whose deistic spirits will from that moment be without compass or direction, anxious for an ideal, but without knowing where to render its adoration, will receive the true light through the universal manifestation of the pure doctrine of Lucifer, brought finally out in the public view. This manifestation will result from the general reactionary movement which will follow the destruction of Christianity and atheism, both conquered and exterminated at the same time."[163]

The drama you're seeing with countries like N. Korea and Iran exists because they haven't agreed to a Rothschild central bank

---

[163] https://www.infowars.com/the-world-wars-of-albert-pike/

yet. You saw Gaddafi get taken out of power in recent history over in Libya. He didn't have a Rothschild bank, neither did Saddam Hussein. Both of those countries do now! Those wars were all about corporate takeover of countries that they hadn't taken over yet. Libya, Iraq, Afghanistan and the drug trade, etc. They usually only use war as their last-ditch effort. They try to trick countries worldwide into accepting huge loans that they can never possibly repay, and just as soon as they fail to repay the loan, the USA comes in and takes over all their assets, oil for example, and set up factories there, basically stealing the country's oil from that point forward, just like what you saw in the Africa example earlier, and they do that worldwide. It's all about consolidating power and gaining more and more control. The first step is the huge loan; if the small country won't accept a "loan" then they'll have the CIA go in an arrange either an assassination or a coup of some kind, to take over power that way. If they can't arrange a coup or assassination, which is what happened with Saddam Hussein because he had such fantastic security, then they'll go to war to get what they want. N. Korea and Iran have been in step three for many years.

> "Economic hit men (EHMs) are highly paid professionals who cheat countries around the globe out of trillions of dollars. They funnel money from the World Bank, the U.S. Agency for International Development (USAID), and other foreign 'aid' organizations into the coffers of huge corporations and the pockets of a few wealthy families who control the planet's natural resources. Their tools include fraudulent financial reports, rigged elections, payoffs, extortion, sex, and murder. They play a game as old as empire, but one that has taken on new and terrifying dimensions during the time of globalization. I should know. I was an EHM." - **John Perkins**[164]

Their extermination compounds, the children's hospitals, are in plain view. Little kids are put to death in open public view, and nobody cares. Those innocent children are 1) given cancer in their vaccines and 2) put to death immediately thereafter with chemotherapy. Nobody bats an eye. Never mind the long list of successful treatments and proven natural cures that have been hidden by your government for over 100 years![165] They've been brainwashed to accept chemotherapy as a medicine the whole time watching innocent people being put to death with it and don't realize what they're seeing. It takes a while, three years or longer sometimes,

---

[164] *Confessions of an Economic Hitman* by John Perkins

[165] www.thetruthaboutcancer.com

but rarely more than five. The fake commercials pleading for help on the TV for these children in these hospitals certainly makes me fume. They're showing pictures of innocent children, all bald and white because they're being systematically poisoned to death by the state, as the announcer pleads you to send money to their fake institution.

> "Never mind the natural methods that we could be using to cure these children for real! We can't make any money off of those methods! We'll just poison them to death and beg the public for more money instead! Please help us now! VISA/MasterCard! Thank you for helping the **Poison the Children Foundation**! We appreciate your kind support."

Hypnosis works really well! The population is clearly brainwashed. All who disagree with what I'm saying about cancer and chemotherapy are definitely victims of their mind-control! Time to wake up now! All that is done by allowing chemotherapy to be used is guaranteeing imminent death. Failing to research anything and then allowing yourselves and/or your children to be put to death by the state really isn't too bright. There are, in fact, other options.[166] Are you going to let the Illuminati kill you with that stuff? When the time comes are you going to say something like the following?

> "Sure thing, go ahead doc. Kill me with that nitrogen mustard gas now. Let's ignore all of the proven cures that are being systematically suppressed. I ignore that information because I'm a patriotic American. Which arm would you like to pump that stuff into, doc? The left or the right?"

They're putting chemicals in everything along with toxins in our food, water, air and medicine because they're bringing the population down and building a New World Order.[167] When you watch the following speech on *YouTube* pay close attention to Bush's eyes as he gives the speech. Look at the cold stare.

---

[166] www.thetruthaboutcancer.com

[167] *New World Order: The Ancient Plan of Secret Societies* by William T. Still

"We have before us the opportunity to forge for ourselves and for future generations, a New World Order, a world where the rule of law, not the law of the jungle, governs the conduct of nations. When we are successful, and we will be, we have a real chance at this New World Order, an order in which a credible United Nations can use its peacekeeping role to fulfill the promising vision of the UN's founders." - **George H.W. Bush**[168]

In this society money is God and people aren't people, they're numbers. Quite literally, your birth certificate is a certificate of stock, and your parents are registering you as a corporation. If you look, you'll notice that your name is written in ALL CAPITAL LETTERS on official documents. There's a reason for that; it's because you're a corporation not a human to them. When you go out and work, they issue you a taxpayer ID # called a Social Security Number. Again, to them you're just a number! People are objects to be used for the purpose of extracting money and profiting. Nothing else. If they don't have any money, they are worthless to the system. The system only caters to people with money, credit and/or a good health insurance plan so that their profit machine can keep rolling. If you don't have money, they won't even give you your medicine, they'll tell you to leave. Humane treatment of human beings is beyond their comprehension. If they can't get anything out of us, they throw us away. If you don't have any money you're scum, you're worthless, get the fuck out of here. That's the American way.

"It's all about money, not freedom. You think you're free? Try going somewhere without money." - **Bill Hicks**

According to many Americans, being "too political" is a terrible offense. According to these people, if you care about the world enough to get involved then you're just far too negative of a

---

[168] https://youtu.be/8DtEcZ3cfg4

person, especially if what you post goes against the government's official line, then they'll hate your guts even more. It's apparently much better to just ignore the problems of the world like they do, as far as they're concerned. If you have the facts on your side, they'll call you a bully rather than accept the information as true.

> "You need to stop using the facts to be a jerk so much!" - **Random** *FaceBook* **comment that I received**

The person above completely acknowledges that I'm presenting factually proven contents, but then simultaneously calls me a jerk. I get it; I'm a jerk for telling the truth. That's the clear message. They'll leave you rude comments and block you. They'd rather be ignorant and avoid any and all involvement and discussion. They turn a blind eye and a deaf ear and then scold people like me for posting factually true and correct information. I'm not supposed to do that, it's too negative they say. Why are they resisting information that can help them? Why resist info that could save their children's lives? Are they brainwashed? Clearly. Even when I'm posting up cures for cancer[169] they go ignored by the thousands of people that I present them to. Common sense and logic says to follow the evidence where it leads, you don't avoid it like the plague and you never, ever deny it, you embrace it! Why? Because the truth is never the opposite of the facts, it's always in alignment with them! Facts and evidence are the only true authority, all else is hearsay and unverified information. In the world of logic if you have a claim that you're examining, but none of it can be verified true, you can't claim it to be true. Not without proper evidence. That's not allowed. Lack of evidence means that it's not verified, therefore if you claim it to be true, you're a liar because your claim has no factual backing. Simply saying that it's so doesn't make it so. Empty claims aren't permissible. Only evidence is permitted in the world of logic. Ignoring factually proven evidence that contradicts what you choose to believe isn't allowed either. That makes you a liar too, because you're omitting things. Omitting things so that you can lie about a verdict doesn't fly. If you're fair and balanced, all sides are considered equally, without bias. Ignoring one side while embracing the other is 100% anti-productive as well as dishonest. Only mind-

---

[169] www.cancertutor.com

controlled slaves do that. When we're being logical and using common sense, all of the evidence from all angles and viewpoints needs to be considered. We take all available factual information and we put it on the table. Only after we've considered the entire body of evidence do we proceed in making an evaluation. If all available evidence isn't considered, if you've omitted some evidence, then any verdict or conclusion that you've arrived at becomes null and void. Try again. This time use all of the evidence instead of ignoring what you so conveniently like to avoid! Logic doesn't allow for bias. And that's very bad news for typical Americans because they rely on bias, it's their lifeblood. They thrive on blindly believing bullshit.

<u>AMERICAN BULLSHIT</u>
by George Carlin

"America's leading industry, America's most profitable business, is still the manufacture, packaging, distribution and marketing of bullshit. High-quality, grade-A, prime-cut, pure, American bullshit. And the sad part is, that most people seem to have been indoctrinated to believe that bullshit only comes from certain places, certain sources: advertising, politics, salesmen – not true. Bullshit is everywhere. Bullshit is rampant. Parents are full of shit, teachers are full of shit, clergymen are full of shit, and law enforcement people are full...of...shit – this entire country. This entire country is completely full of shit, and always has been. From the Declaration of Independence to the Constitution to the Star-Spangled Banner, it's still nothing more than one big steaming pile of red, white and blue, all-American bullshit. Because, think of how we started. Think of that. This country was founded by a group of slave-owners who told us all men are created equal. Oh yeah, all men, except for Indians and niggers and women, right? I always like to use that authentic American language. This was a small group of unelected, white, male, land-holding, slave-owners who also suggested their class be the only one allowed to vote. Now, that is what's known as being stunningly and embarrassingly full of shit. And I think Americans really show their ignorance when they say they want their politicians to be honest. What are these fuckin' cretins talking about? If honesty were suddenly introduced into American life, the whole system would collapse!"

The Ten Commandments of Logic

1: Thou shalt not attack the person's character, but instead prove the argument itself incorrect. (**Ad Hominem**)

2: Thou shalt not misrepresent or exaggerate a person's argument in order to make it easier to attack. (**Straw Man Fallacy**)

3: Thou shalt not use small minorities to represent the whole. (**Hasty Generalization**)

4: Thou shalt not argue thy position by assuming one of it's premises is true. (**Begging the Question**)

5: Thou shalt not claim that because something occurred before, it must be the cause. (**Post Hoc/False Cause**)

6: Thou shalt not reduce the argument down to two possibilities. (**False Dichotomy**)

7: Thou shalt not argue that because of our ignorance, the claim must be true or false. (**Ad Ignorantiam**)

8: Thou shalt not lay the burden of proof onto the person who's questioning the claim. (**Burden of Proof**)

9: Thou shalt not assume "this" follows "that" when it has no logical connection. (**Non sequitur**)

10: Thou shalt not claim that because a claim is popular it must be true. (**Bandwagon Fallacy**)

THE PREVIOUS CHAPTER IS ALL SUPPORTED WITH VERIFIED FACTS AND EMPIRICAL SCIENCE but don't worry, I think *American Idol* comes on at 7:00 pm! Enjoy your next appointment at the pediatrician's office with your kids and remember what I said in this book concerning vaccines—your child's life depends on it!

"Truth will ultimately prevail where there is pains to bring it to light." - **George Washington**[170]

This book's author can be contacted at **AKTAR@activist.com**

Visit the Light Warrior blog online: http://sites.google.com/site/aktarlightwarrior

---

[170] Exactly as quoted by Donald Trump on *Twitter*

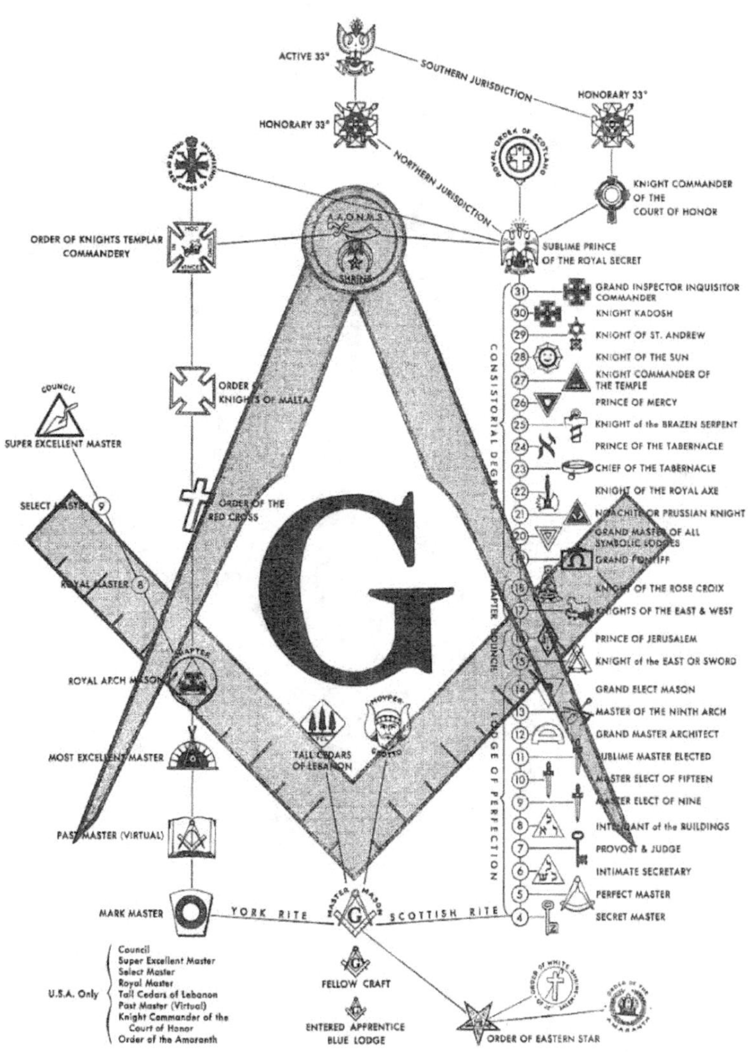

www.ingramcontent.com/pod-product-compliance
Lightning Source LLC
Chambersburg PA
CBHW050923260726
48660CB00001B/362